THE HOLY SPIRIT MY SENIOR PARTNER

DAVID YONGGI CHO

Charisma
HOUSE
A STRANG COMPANY

THE HOLY SPIRIT, MY SENIOR PARTNER by Paul Yonggi Cho
Published by Charisma House
A Strang Company
600 Rinehart Road
Lake Mary, FL 32746
www.charismahouse.com

Unless otherwise noted, all Scripture references are from the
King James Version of the Bible.

Library of Congress Catalog Card Number: 88-64193
International Standard Book Number: 0-88419-226-1

04 05 06 07 — 24 23 22
Printed in the United States of America

Contents

Introduction

God's divine executive agent in the world today is the Holy Spirit. He is continuing the work that Jesus began. He is moving among millions of believers and unbelievers all over the world—in homes, churches and prisons, behind the Iron and Bamboo Curtains, and in countries where the gospel has been resisted for centuries. He is moving and working in response to the pleas of God's children everywhere. His work is powerful and continues steadily in the lives of Christians who have sought His help. Christians who have developed a steady and growing prayer life, and who communicate and fellowship with the Spirit, are those who know Jesus Christ the best.

The Holy Spirit can never be underestimated. He is always in control of situations that have been given to Him in prayer.

THE HOLY SPIRIT, MY SENIOR PARTNER

In split seconds He has intervened to divert disasters, to reveal the right decisions to make, to help Christians through the most critical circumstances. He has alerted believers, even when separated by thousands of miles, to pray or be available to assist Him when necessary. He has asked others to pray for a need weeks before the need surfaced. The busiest executives around the world would pay any price to have a senior partner like Him.

I began pastoring while I was still attending a small Assemblies of God Bible college in Seoul. In the aftermath of the Korean conflict, the despair of the people was so evident I realized that those who desired to minister to them needed a supernatural ability to rise above the problems, sickness and poverty.

I prayed for an experience with the Holy Spirit whom I had studied and learned about. I asked the Holy Spirit to come and fill me with His power, His ministry and His message for a sick and hurting world. I realized that by myself I could never find enough uplifting and encouraging sermons to preach unless I lived above my own problems. So daily I prayed for the filling of the Holy Spirit. Other students were also praying for this baptism of the Holy Spirit. We prayed for days, and as fellow students received this experience, I noticed their lives took on a new dimension. They were still poor, but in their poverty they were full of joy and peace with an unexplainable confidence that God was going to help them. Problems did not disturb their peace. As I observed the change in their lives, I knew I had to keep praying until I received this experience also.

And then it happened. One evening while I was asking the Lord for the filling of the Holy Spirit, I felt His presence draw near. It was a wonderful experience. I was worshipping and praising Jesus aloud, telling Him audibly again and again how wonderful it was to know Him and how much I loved Him. Though I could not see anyone, it seemed as if the Holy Spirit stood before me, ready to pour a blessing upon me.

As I worshipped, I felt a warm glow touch my face, then my tongue, then my body, and without realizing it I began to speak new words that came to my mind and my tongue at the same time. The more I spoke, the more I felt impressed to speak forth the words that were coming so quickly. I don't know how long I remained in that room worshipping the Lord, and it didn't matter. My heart was overflowing with praise and worship to Jesus in a new language. I was overwhelmed with joy and an awareness of a new power with God that I had not known before.

That was my initial experience when I was baptized with the Holy Spirit. Every day after that, I felt I was living in the very presence of Jesus. It was difficult for me to explain it. Each time I prayed, the Holy Spirit came to help me pray, taking my Korean language and substituting for it a heavenly language I had never learned. I knew my spirit had become one with Him, and I could pray for a whole hour or more with greater ease.

After graduating from Bible college, I felt I should start a church. The Holy Spirit impressed upon me where and how to begin, and I recognized His help in those decisions. I purchased a used army tent and pitched it in a slum area among needy families.

Everything did not go perfectly from that day to this, but I began to learn how much the Holy Spirit was interested in helping me develop the ministry that He Himself had given me. No matter how wonderful our experiences with the Lord have been, we are still in the flesh. As long as we seek counsel from the Lord, we will receive it. But it is so easy to evaluate a situation and think, I can do this by myself, so I will not trouble the Lord in prayer or ask the Holy Spirit to help me.

Without fully realizing what I had done, I formulated my own plans for the new tent church. I wanted the program to be impressive and many people to come, but I struggled to make sermons. When I couldn't do very well, I gathered all the sermons by Billy Graham and Oral Roberts that I could find and preached them. The problem was that I soon ran out of sermons and was right back where I started. At times I became discouraged and wanted to quit. At this point in my young ministry, I returned to prayer and asked the Holy Spirit to help me.

Letting the Holy Spirit direct one's life is not always easy. Self gets in the way even in preparing a sermon; one can choose good Scripture verses and make a sermon—and leave the Holy Spirit completely out of the process. How many times I had to confess my sin of trying to do everything by myself! Then I would invite Him to come again and help me. And each time the Holy Spirit helped me—even to prepare sermons. Sometimes the message was totally different from what I had prepared. He gave me His thoughts and the Scripture verses He wanted me to share, because He knew who would be present in those meetings and their needs.

I returned to the Scriptures often and read that the Holy Spirit came to abide with us forever (see John 14:16); to bring all things to our remembrance that He said to us in the Word (see John 14:26); to testify of Jesus (see John 15:26); to guide us into all truth (see John 16:13); to show us things to come (see John 16:13); and to glorify Jesus in everything and show that glory to believers (see John 16:14).

One day the Holy Spirit spoke to my heart: "If you want your church to grow, you must develop a greater communion and fellowship with Me. Don't preach about the Holy Spirit as an experience only. He is an awesome person! Preach about the person. Develop a communion and fellowship by waiting in My presence after prayer. I want to talk to you also."

After I was married, there was a time when my wife was very unhappy. I had been busy in evangelistic meetings during the week and came home on Saturday to rest and prepare to preach in my church on Sunday. I would bring home a suitcase of dirty clothes and replenish my supply for another week. Every time my wife would try to share something with me or talk about the happenings of her week, I would always apologize that I had to study, or I had to pray, or I had to do something else. I didn't take time to sit and visit as I had when we were dating. "After all," I stated without feeling, "God has called me to preach, and I'm very busy preparing sermons. You have a baby to keep you company and a home to take care of. What more do you want?"

One day my mother-in-law came to visit and said she wanted to talk with me. In those days I was always afraid when she said she wanted to talk with me because that meant I was not doing something right. "Do you love your wife?" she asked.

"Yes, of course," I answered.

"Then you must spend some time with her as well as with your ministry. She is not a thing. She is a person. She is happy when you recognize her and talk with her, and she feels rejected when you don't."

That day I learned a great lesson about love relationships. I began to show my love for my wife in many ways. I took time to talk with her about our home and our baby. We made a plan to take Mondays off together and she would outline our day. The smile returned to her face. At the evening meal, she presented me with her plans. We were going to the park for our first Monday morning and have lunch out. Those plans developed just as she wanted and we did the things that made her happy. In no time, my home life turned around. I had a happy and satisfied wife again, which made me happy when

I left the following week for more gospel meetings.

Through that experience I learned a tremendous lesson. My understanding of the Holy Spirit changed. He, too, is a person who needs fellowship. Otherwise, He is grieved. Instead of praying and hurrying off to the church, I took time to sit in His presence and let Him talk with me. Since He gave me the ministry I have, and since He desired to lead and guide me into ways to fulfill that ministry, I looked forward to the times of talking with Him. I conversed with Him as a friend talks with a friend, as a husband talks with his wife—talking and listening and remembering.

As the weeks passed, I understood the ministry of the Holy Spirit better than ever. He is a faithful friend who came to do all that the Word declares He would do. I asked Him to be my senior partner in everything that concerned my life and God's work.

Every morning since then, when I awake I say, "Good morning, Holy Spirit. Let's work together today and I will be Your vessel." Every evening before retiring I say again, "It's been a wonderful day working with You, Holy Spirit. Cover my family and me with Your divine protection as we rest through the night." The next morning again I greet Him as a person and invite Him to go with me through the day and take the lead in all affairs that must be handled, and He does.

When it is time to prepare sermons, He is always present. When I am counseling, He is directing my counsel to each individual. When I am making a decision—which preaching invitations should I accept?—He guides me. Why? Because He watches over the needs and situations of every area of the world, and He knows which area is ready for the words He has prepared me to preach. As I walk to the pulpit, I say, "Let's go, Holy Spirit. You're on!" When the meeting is over and

I return home (or to my hotel if I am preaching abroad), I tell Him, "Thank You, Senior Partner. You did a great work in the hearts of people tonight. Keep working. Encourage those pastors through the new converts who found You tonight." And when He has free rein in the service, His presence makes the difference.

Have you ever stood on top of a mountain and observed how small everything seemed below? When you have received the fullness of the Holy Spirit, you will almost immediately notice that life's problems and your personal needs also seem very small—because you are looking at them from a different perspective. You are seeing them as the Holy Spirit does, because He is in control.

As you read this book, I trust you will meet the Holy Spirit personally in its pages. He wants to be your senior partner, too. When you develop that close communion with Him, He will make a difference in your business, your family relationships, your decision making—in every area of your life.

The weeks and months have rolled by, and I am completing thirty years of ministry. I have seen many miracles of healing, interventions in church situations and unusual answers to prayer. God has raised up many leaders in our church who have gone on to be outstanding missionaries and pastors. If I were to assess what I have learned since my conversion, I would say meeting the Holy Spirit and learning to know Him in an intimate way has been the greatest experience of my life. My senior partner and I are still very close, and we fellowship every day!

David Yonggi Cho
Senior Pastor
Yoido Full Gospel Church
Seoul, Korea

1

Communion With the Holy Spirit—Why?

In 2 Corinthians 13:14, Paul wrote a benediction to the believers in Corinth: "The grace of the Lord Jesus Christ, and the love of God, and the communion of the Holy Ghost, be with you all."

What deep feelings that benediction stirs within me. But I find that's not true with everyone. The countless blessings these words can bestow are disappearing from hearts today. A little later on I'll get to the why behind that statement, but first let me describe what the blessings are.

The Grace of Christ

The original meaning of the Greek word for *grace* was "the ultimate in beauty." The Greeks enjoyed the pursuit of

15

beauty—through philosophy and sports, poetry and drama, sculpture and architecture. And of course their land—mountains and streams and coastline—surrounded them with beauty. When the beauty of something gave joy to the viewer or hearer, the Greeks said it was full of grace. Eventually, this meaning developed a broader sense, to include not only the beauty of things but also beautiful works, acts, thoughts, eloquence and even mankind—all could be considered full of grace.

A second meaning of *grace* was "favor," good will given out of unconditional, overflowing love with no expectation of reward or payment.

A third meaning of *grace* referred to a praiseworthy work, exhibiting virtues far exceeding the common.

In his benediction, the apostle Paul must have felt a surging joy beyond description, knowing the unconditional forgiveness of sins and the many blessings of salvation—full of beauty or grace.

The Love of God

How should we accept the following benediction, "the love of God...be with you all"? Have we become so hardened that we can hear about the love of God without being moved or having a contrite heart? Almost any Christian today can quote John 3:16, yet only the letters remain, the life in them having been forgotten.

There are several kinds of love, including the parental love for children of one's own flesh and blood, the love that longs for and yearns after the opposite sex, and the fraternal love which gives us joy when we fellowship with dear friends. But human love can by no means be compared to the love of God. Parental love is limited to children. The love between the sexes is self-centered. Even the love between friends will falter if

16

one never receives anything in return for care and concern. But the love of God is different.

Divine love in the Greek language refers to a love that wholly sacrifices itself for the object of its love, realizing the precious value of it. For example, man and woman betrayed God and fell into deep sin resulting in an abominable life, which ultimately led to eternal destruction. In spite of this betrayal, God lovingly sacrificed Himself on Calvary to save mankind. Why? Because each individual soul is priceless to Him. This is divine love!

Though in a fallen state of sin, mankind possesses the image of God and we can become noble creatures if we receive the grace of redemption.

God is love and His love is true love. He loved the sinners of this world so much that He didn't even spare His only Son, but made Him a sacrifice for our sins. Is it not true love that He loved even us who are fallen in sin? Paul was probably moved to tears when he wrote of the love of God, but why have we become so cold?

How can our faith be restored so that we can be deeply moved by the grace of Jesus Christ and the love of God? Where is the path to restoration? Indeed, there is a way to full restoration. There is an answer to the cry of our spirits, and it is found in the communion of the Holy Spirit. The Holy Spirit pours all grace and love into our spirits through His communion with us.

The Communion of the Holy Spirit

Communion means "communicating with or traveling together, transporting with." The splendid development of transportation has made the modern world a global town. Through this rapid and convenient transportation, people all over the world share what is needed to meet their cultural, political, economic, military and scientific needs. It is not an exaggeration to say that you can measure a civilization by the development of its transportation system.

Suppose this global system of transportation were suddenly brought to a standstill. The whole world would become a living hell. Almost every kind of work would ultimately be paralyzed. Cities would suffer from hunger and cold, as food and fuel supplies would stop. Rural areas and factories would become heaped with decaying farm products and commodities, as marketing channels would be clogged. Transportation is no dispensable convenience. It is necessary to human welfare. Likewise, the communion of the Holy Spirit—daily traveling and constant fellowship with the Holy Spirit—is essential for our spiritual well-being.

The measure of our faith is in direct proportion to our communion with the Holy Spirit. Through the communion of the Holy Spirit, we receive spiritual blessings and we tell Him our earnest desires. Though the grace of Jesus Christ and the love of God may abound immeasurably in heaven, they are useless to us if they do not reach us. Likewise, though our hearts are full of earnest desires, if the Holy Spirit does not help us commune with God through prayer, we cannot pray properly.

The Bible confirms this fact clearly. "The Lord direct your hearts into the love of God, and into the patient waiting for Christ" (2 Thess. 3:5).

In this verse, "the Lord" refers to the Holy Spirit, as He is the One who leads us into the love of God and into the patient waiting for Christ. However abundant the grace of Jesus Christ and the love of God are, if the Holy Spirit does not lead our hearts into such grace and love, our faith is merely the faith of dead words. If the Holy Spirit does not help us commune with God, our prayer will be like that of the Pharisees, totally lacking in life.

The Bible clearly teaches that the Spirit assists us in our praying: "The Spirit also helpeth our infirmities: for we know not what we should pray for as we ought: but the Spirit itself maketh intercession for us with groanings which cannot be uttered" (Rom. 8:26). Jude 20 also points out the Spirit's place in our prayer life: "Beloved, building up yourselves on your most holy faith, praying in the Holy Ghost."

The word *communion*, as used by Paul in his Corinthian benediction, "the communion of the Holy Ghost be with you all," has deep implications. The Greek word has two important meanings.

Fellowship

The first meaning refers to intercourse or fellowship on the basis of intimate friendship. Without fellowship with the Holy Spirit there can be no spiritual life, no faith with power and victory. The early church was abundant with fervent prayer, overflowing passion, rich vitality and thanksgiving, gushing out like a spring as a result of their fellowship with the Holy Spirit. Why are Christians settling for mere outward formalities of religion, dry ceremonies of worship, seeing the church as a place of social intercourse? This emptiness has left young people sick of the Christian way and its form of godliness. They have become disillusioned—because the church has lost its spiritual life!

John A. Mackey, former dean of Princeton University's theological college and Presbyterian Alliance Theological Seminary, said in a Presbyterian meeting: "It is better to approach religion with natural feelings than to come to it with aesthetic and orderly forms without dynamic power. One of the most important problems the church of today faces is that it regards it lawful to express feelings in every field but religion.

What the present church needs is to provide something which will inflame all the human passions. From the very moment the church is completely programized [sic] and depersonalized, it becomes merely a memorial of God instead of the living institution of the power of God.''

What is the answer to the problem he points out? Fervent fellowship with the living Holy Spirit. Without it, the church naturally becomes cold; worship becomes mechanical. Faith loses the burning passion which gives a depth to our whole personality. This kind of faith is like a stove with no fire.

Knowing this, the first question the apostle Paul asked some Ephesians who appeared tired and dejected was: "Have ye received the Holy Ghost since ye believed?" (Acts 19:2). When Jesus saw His disciples were in sorrow and despair, He promised the Holy Spirit would come and abide in their spirits: "I will pray the Father, and he shall give you another Comforter, that he may abide with you for ever...I will not leave you comfortless: I will come to you" (John 14:16,18).

That comfort can be ours, but in more cases than we realize, believers today have not even heard about the Holy Spirit.

How do we have fellowship with the Holy Spirit? First, we must acknowledge that He is present in His church and welcome Him, earnestly desiring His guidance and opening our hearts to depend upon Him continually. The love of God and the grace of Jesus can reach our spirits only through fellowship and communion with the Holy Spirit.

Partnership in Evangelism

The second meaning of *communion* is "to do business in partnership" (see Luke 5:10) and "to participate in" (see 2 Cor. 10:16; Phil. 3:10)—to work together as partners for the same purpose and to share joy, sorrow, victory and trials.

The Holy Spirit was sent to this earth for the very purpose

20

of working in partnership with believers, to quicken dead spirits by witnessing to the grace of Jesus Christ. Before He left this world, Jesus said to His disciples, "When the Comforter is come, whom I will send unto you from the Father, even the Spirit of truth, which proceedeth from the Father, he shall testify of me: And ye also shall bear witness, because ye have been with me from the beginning" (John 15:26,27).

From this, we can understand that the great mission of preaching the gospel was first given to the Holy Spirit and then to the saints who believed in the Lord. But Jesus emphasized here that the work of evangelism should be carried out as a partnership between the Holy Spirit and mankind—with the Holy Spirit participating as the senior partner. We can conclude that the whole reason why evangelism today makes so little progress, why the church is retrograde in the work of winning souls and why it has been on the brink of bankruptcy is that this partnership with the Holy Spirit has been broken. These days, people neither acknowledge the Holy Spirit nor welcome Him. Since they don't depend upon Him, they end up in failure, trying to accomplish the work of God through their own means and efforts.

This tragic failure was clearly pointed out in the book of Revelation: "Behold, I stand at the door, and knock: if any man hear my voice, and open the door, I will come in to him, and will sup with him, and he with me" (3:20).

If these words had been addressed to the unbelieving world, they would not be surprising. But they were given to the Laodicean church, the believers in the end time of the world. What a horrible revelation!

Think of it. Our Lord said He would be with us forever through the Holy Spirit, yet the church is trying to do the work of God through human-centered worship, driving out the

Holy Spirit and leaving Him outside the door!

It was not so in the early church. The first-century saints realized that evangelism should be done from beginning to end in partnership with the Holy Spirit.

When the preaching apostles were taken to be examined before the Jewish council in Jerusalem, Peter answered the council's questions thus:

> The God of our fathers raised up Jesus, whom ye slew and hanged on a tree. Him hath God exalted with his right hand to be a Prince and a Saviour, for to give repentance to Israel, and forgiveness of sins. And we are his witnesses of these things; and so is also the Holy Ghost, whom God hath given to them that obey Him (Acts 5:30-32).

There Peter confirmed that the apostles' work of evangelism was carried out in partnership with the Holy Spirit.

Jesus did not begin to preach the kingdom of heaven until after He had received the fullness of the Holy Spirit. Only then was He able to complete His ministry in three-and-a-half years with great power and authority. Realizing this, how dare we think we could accomplish the work of God with only human power and wisdom?

A young man named Archibald Brown once entered a pastor's college established by the world-renowned preacher C.H. Spurgeon. After Brown graduated from that school, he became a highly successful pastor in London and thousands of people flocked to hear his preaching. Many admired the tremendous anointing on the young minister and wondered where his great power came from. After he died, the secret was found in the old, well-thumbed Bible he had used. At Acts 15:28 he had penned a footnote: "Ah, how important is a partnership with the senior partner, the Holy Spirit! Without His partnership, no life of faith or evangelical work has value.''

The blessing and success in our life of faith and gospel preaching are also in direct proportion to the depth of our fellowship with our senior partner, the Holy Spirit.

After His resurrection and before His ascension, Jesus gathered His disciples about Him and gravely commanded them to preach the gospel to the whole world: ''Go ye therefore, and teach all nations, baptizing them in the name of the Father, and of the Son, and of the Holy Ghost: Teaching them to observe all things whatsoever I have commanded you: and, lo, I am with you alway, even unto the end of the world'' (Matt. 28:19,20).

But after the Lord said this, He didn't tell them to begin preaching at once. He told them that the preaching of the gospel could not be done without partnership with the Holy Spirit: ''Behold, I send the promise of my Father upon you: but tarry ye in the city of Jerusalem, until ye be endued with power from on high'' (Luke 24:49). ''John truly baptized with water; but ye shall be baptized with the Holy Ghost not many days hence....Ye shall receive power, after that the Holy Ghost is come upon you: and ye shall be witnesses unto me'' (Acts 1:5,8).

The wonderful victory of the gospel in the early church happened because the disciples wholly obeyed Jesus' commandment. They tarried in Jerusalem until they were filled with the Holy Spirit, and then they preached.

G. Campbell Morgan, an English theologian and successful pastor, wrote this commentary on Acts 5:30-32:

> The witness of the Holy Spirit is the only eventual power of the church. Among other factors this is the most powerful truth of all. If we cannot cooperate well with the Holy Spirit, we cannot exercise an influence of the

gospel in Jerusalem or in London. If those who preach the gospel are not empowered with this invisible power and the church does not reflect to the world this eternal and mysterious light it has received, both of them will always be lacking, good for nothing and as cold as death, though their outward appearance seems to be spotlessly perfect and just fine. If we really want to fill London with the Holy Spirit, we should by all means do our business in partnership with the Holy Spirit. If we only do that, the church will continuously march toward successive victories with God through joy and trial.

In the book of Acts, it was written clearly and repeatedly that the gospel was preached in partnership with the Holy Spirit.

In Acts 8, we meet deacon Philip, who went down to Samaria and led revival meetings at which a great multitude of people repented and were saved. Countless people were healed. Great miracles and wonders were performed and joy abounded. In the midst of this great revival, an angel suddenly appeared to Philip and told him to go south, toward Gaza.

How different God's will is from man's. It would *seem* that the devil had tempted Philip with a wrong revelation. Why should he have left those victorious meetings to go to a desolate wilderness? Because Philip did his business in partnership with the Holy Spirit. He was sure that this order was truly given by the Spirit Himself. In obedience, he left the Samaritan meetings and went out to the wilderness by faith, not knowing where he was going. But the Holy Spirit had planned the deliverance of the whole African continent through the deliverance of one Ethiopian soul whom Philip would encounter!

The Bible describes the scene this way: ''And he [Philip] arose and went: and, behold, a man of Ethiopia, an eunuch of great authority under Candace, queen of the Ethiopians, who had the charge of all her treasure, and had come to Jerusalem for to worship, was returning, and sitting in his chariot read Esaias the prophet'' (Acts 8:27,28).

The Holy Spirit sent Philip to the desert to preach the gospel of salvation to one prepared soul. And because this one Ethiopian was saved, Philip came to reap a harvest far greater than he would have reaped had he remained in Samaria leading gospel meetings. We should neither neglect nor despise what seem to be small leadings of the Holy Spirit; we have no idea what He might have planned.

The Holy Spirit's word to Philip became even more specific: ''The Spirit said unto Philip, Go near, and join thyself to this chariot'' (Acts 8:29).

Led by the invisible Holy Spirit, Philip approached the chariot at the right time and place when the Ethiopian eunuch was reading Isaiah 53, the prophecy of Christ's suffering for our atonement. What wonderful guidance and appropriate timing it was. After hearing Philip's preaching, the Ethiopian received Jesus as Savior. When they came upon a place where there was water, he was baptized.

What took place afterward shows how powerful partnership with the Holy Spirit in the work of preaching the gospel can be: ''And when they were come up out of the water, the Spirit of the Lord caught away Philip, that the eunuch saw him no more: and he went on his way rejoicing'' (Acts 8:39).

The Spirit of the Lord ''caught away Philip.'' That's some partnership.

Some might justify their powerlessness with an excuse that the Holy Spirit does not work in such a way today. But Jesus said concerning the Holy Spirit, ''He [the Father] shall give you another Comforter, that he may abide with you *for ever*'' (John 14:16, italics mine).

25

THE HOLY SPIRIT, MY SENIOR PARTNER

The Holy Spirit is the same forever and He is with us at this moment. If the Holy Spirit is not able to work it is because believers today betray and deny Him, and do not depend upon Him and pay heed to Him. Neglect of the Holy Spirit is what makes the powerful gospel become old news, like antiques in a museum.

In Acts 10, we find another scene of partnership. Peter in partnership with the Holy Spirit is sent to preach to a Gentile centurion, named Cornelius, and his entire house:

> Peter went up upon the housetop to pray about the sixth hour: And he became very hungry, and would have eaten: but while they made ready, he fell into a trance, and saw heaven opened, and a certain vessel descending unto him, as it had been a great sheet knit at the four corners, and let down to the earth: Wherein were all manner of fourfooted beasts of the earth, and wild beasts, and creeping things, and fowls of the air. And there came a voice to him, Rise, Peter; kill and eat. But Peter said, Not so, Lord; for I have never eaten any thing that is common or unclean. And the voice spake unto him again the second time, What God hath cleansed, that call not thou common. This was done thrice: and the vessel was received up again into heaven. Now while Peter doubted in himself what this vision which he had seen should mean, behold, the men which were sent from Cornelius had made enquiry for Simon's house, and stood before the gate, and called and asked whether Simon, which was surnamed Peter, were lodged there. While Peter thought on the vision, the Spirit said unto him, Behold, three men seek thee. Arise therefore, and get thee down, and go with them, doubting nothing: for I have sent them (Acts 10:9-20).

Here once again, we can understand that the Holy Spirit works for the deliverance of souls. Cornelius, a centurion of the Roman army in Caesarea, was a devout man, but he had not yet received salvation. God's Holy Spirit, through the message of an angel, instructed Cornelius to send for Peter as the vessel to preach the gospel (see vv. 1-8). Peter, raised a devout Jew, abhorred companionship, even conversation, with Gentiles, who were "unclean" according to Jewish law. But in order to broaden the sphere of Peter's ministry, the Holy Spirit made Peter see a strange vision—three times—and then He ordered Peter not to doubt, but to go to the house of the Gentile Cornelius.

What a wonderful ministry of the Holy Spirit! He had prepared both parties—the messenger and the one who received the message. It is beyond our comprehension how desperately such a ministry of the Holy Spirit is needed today—to send a prepared vessel to a prepared spirit. God is the only one who knows the right timing.

When Peter was preaching the gospel in the house of Cornelius, he said, "He commanded us to preach unto the people, and to testify that it is he which was ordained of God to be the Judge of quick and dead. To him give all the prophets witness, that through his name whosoever believeth in him shall receive remission of sins" (vv. 42,43).

The account continues: "While Peter yet spake these words the Holy Ghost fell on all them which heard the word. And they of the circumcision which believed were astonished, as many as came with Peter, because that on the Gentiles also was poured out the gift of the Holy Ghost" (vv. 44,45). Such a wonderful work as this could take place only in partnership with the Holy Spirit.

Later on in Acts, Luke describes a scene in which a whole congregation worked together with the Holy Spirit.

> Now there were in the church that was at Antioch certain prophets and teachers....As they ministered to the Lord, and fasted, the *Holy Ghost said*, Separate me Barnabas and Saul for the work whereunto I have called them. And when they had fasted and prayed, and laid their hands on them, they sent them away (Acts 13:1-4, italics mine).

From this account we can learn several important lessons concerning the relationship between the work of evangelism and the Holy Spirit. In preaching the gospel, the Holy Spirit is omnipotent, sovereign. Here the Holy Spirit shows that He holds the position of preeminence in the church by using the pronoun *I*, which signifies that the work of the gospel is the work that the Holy Spirit demands. Here the Holy Spirit emphasized that the ambassador extraordinary and plenipotentiary is neither a denomination nor any human person, but the Holy Spirit Himself.

This passage also clearly teaches that those who labored in the gospel could accomplish their mission only through partnership with the Holy Spirit. Without earnestly waiting upon the guidance of the Holy Spirit like this church of Antioch, which ministered to the Lord and prayed in the spirit, how could one hear the still small voice of the Holy Spirit?

It is sad but true that the church today is filled with plans and programs for human interest: worship is planned and presented for fleshly pleasure through social association. There is little interest in hearing from the Holy Spirit. As a result, the church, which should be taking care of the work of the kingdom of heaven, has become wasted. It is on the brink of bankruptcy and has become an object of ridicule and reproach!

In every city, town and community there are church buildings, yet the spirits of worshippers have become empty and void.

We have discarded the commandment of the Lord that told us that we should become the light of the world. We have stopped up our ears to the calling of the Holy Spirit. The church, like a flock of lost sheep, wanders to and fro, and falls prey to the devil who walks about seeking whom he may devour. Heresy and false teachings flourish.

In such a whirlpool, when and how could the prayer meetings of Antioch ever be restored to us? At Antioch, didn't they minister with one accord to the Lord as they waited for their divine orders? Didn't they earnestly fast and pray so they could do the work to which the Holy Spirit, their senior partner, had called them? To evangelize the coming age, we should once again go into the bosom of the Holy Spirit who gives us supernatural power, wisdom and guidance. We should repent and open our ears to His calling.

The account of the events at Antioch goes on to say that Barnabas and Saul, who were set apart by the Holy Spirit for His work, "being sent forth by the Holy Ghost, departed" (Acts 13:4).

What a thought-provoking dispatch this was. They left, being sent forth neither by any denomination nor by any missionary institution, but by the Holy Spirit! They had no missionary funds, nor any promise of regular missionary support. Nothing is said about money, yet they were sent forth by the Holy Spirit, the Lord of heaven and earth. With that backing, they had nothing to fear. Of course, it does not mean that neither a denomination nor money nor mission society was needed, but they were not sent by a group of people or an institution.

Senior Theologian

I really wish that all of the churches and institutions engaged in evangelizing the world today would be filled with the Holy Spirit—instead of just being filled with people—so that we could

29

experience the divine victory that can be obtained through the pure gospel. Only this—not humanistic, secularized, defeatist preaching—will release the victory of the gospel message to the world.

Behind the scenes, setting up a sound basis for the work of evangelism, the Holy Spirit was also the early church's senior partner in settling theological questions. Like an unseen stage director, He had final authority to supervise and teach and lead.

In Acts 15, some Gentile Christians were in great confusion because of the false teaching of certain Jewish believers:

> And certain men which came down from Judea taught the brethren, and said, Except ye be circumcised after the manner of Moses, ye cannot be saved. When therefore Paul and Barnabas had no small dissension and disputation with them, they determined that Paul and Barnabas, and certain other of them, should go up to Jerusalem unto the apostles and elders about this question (vv. 1,2).

As a result, the apostles and the elders held a council in Jerusalem to consider this matter.

The council's discussion and verdict are described later in Acts 15. Reading this leads me to believe that these leaders deeply acknowledged the Holy Spirit, depending on Him and praying with a firm faith that He would lead their discussion to arrive at the proper conclusion. Their conclusion was written as a letter to the Gentiles in Antioch, Syria and Cilicia:

> Forasmuch as we have heard, that certain which went out from us have troubled you with words, subverting your souls, saying, Ye must be circumcised, and keep the law: to whom we gave no such commandment: It seemed good unto us, being assembled with one accord,

to send chosen men unto you with our beloved Barnabas and Paul, men that have hazarded their lives for the name of our Lord Jesus Christ....For it seemed good *to the Holy Ghost, and to us,* to lay upon you no greater burden than these necessary things (vv. 23-28, italics mine).

Considering that the Holy Spirit was clearly mentioned first—"it seemed good to the Holy Ghost, and to us" instead of "to us, and the Holy Ghost"—should make those who interpret the Bible on the basis of humanistic faith ashamed of themselves. Do they really acknowledge the Holy Spirit in today's religious conferences? We often hear expressions such as "Superintendent So-and-So and the committee have decided...." We rarely hear the sentiment used in the letter sent by the Jerusalem apostles: "With the help of the Holy Spirit we have decided...." Of course, I do not contend that one should follow every statement with the expression "by the help of the Holy Spirit," but it is deplorable that the phrase is never heard.

Depending on His Help

In all we do, we should acknowledge Him, worship Him, give thanks to Him, continuously depending upon Him. And we should surely remember that the Holy Spirit, sent by heaven to be our senior partner in evangelization and teaching, waits to be *invited* to be that partner with us.

The Bible shows us that ignorance is not the only thing that prevents us from having a partnership with the Holy Spirit. Lack of humility in waiting on the Spirit is also a factor.

Acts 16:6-10 shows that Paul worked in partnership with the Holy Spirit. Of course, Paul was the apostle of apostles, whom God used mightily. But we should also realize that even an apostle as sensitive to the Holy Spirit as Paul was capable of

31

rushing recklessly into something because of his great zeal for preaching the gospel. This is what happened:

> Now when they [Paul and Silas] had gone throughout Phrygia and the region of Galatia, and *were forbidden of the Holy Ghost* to preach the word in Asia, after they were come to Mysia, they assayed to go into Bithynia: but *the Spirit suffered them not* (vv. 6,7, italics mine).

When we read this passage, we feel as if we are seeing Jacob wrestling with the angel of God. The expressions "were forbidden of the Holy Ghost" and "the Spirit suffered them not" are combative. Paul was trying to go forth to preach, and the Holy Spirit was pulling him back. Such vivid scenes in the Bible show us that it was the Holy Spirit who was leading Paul.

It is impossible to grasp fully the tremendous lesson this passage teaches. This wonderful scene shows clearly that the Holy Spirit earnestly wants to take part in the work of the gospel as a partner, and that the initiator of the work is not man or woman but the Holy Spirit. When they are not led easily, the Holy Spirit even uses force to make His saints obey God's plan for His work. The Holy Spirit commands us to do the work of evangelism, and believers are sent forth as workers for the harvest, but He must be the senior partner.

Even Paul, who possessed an almost spotless and perfect character, had some difficulty being led by the Holy Spirit, because of his burning passion and indomitable will. Maybe the reason God allowed Paul to experience "a thorn in the flesh" (see 2 Cor. 12:7) was so that he might sense his weakness and depend wholly upon the Lord.

From this we should learn that we should always seek first the guidance of the Holy Spirit, and have an obedient and broken spirit that can be led by Him as easily as sheep are led by a shepherd. Only then can the gospel really be preached—in partnership with the Holy Spirit. If we try to do so without Him, we will sadden the heart of God, and oppose His plan and providence to save the world. Such a partnership with the Holy Spirit is indispensable to the church.

2

Who Is the Holy Spirit?

Exactly who is this wonderful Holy Spirit of grace? To have fellowship and work together with Him, we must know Him well. Though impersonal metaphors for the Holy Spirit—fire, wind, water, oil, dove and so forth—have a biblical basis, they have been used to such an extent that some people don't really know who He actually is. Let's look at the bedrock truth.

The Holy Spirit Is God

Like God the Father and God the Son, the Holy Spirit is a member of the Godhead. Historically, Arians, Sabellians and Socinians regarded the Holy Spirit as a power that came from the eternal God, but these groups have always been branded heretics by the orthodox church.

THE HOLY SPIRIT, MY SENIOR PARTNER

The Bible itself calls the Holy Spirit God. Among the things Jesus commanded His disciples to do just before His ascension was: "Go ye therefore, and teach all nations, baptizing them in the name of the Father, and of the Son, and of the Holy Ghost" (Matt. 28:19). Here Jesus clearly set the Holy Spirit in the same position as the Father and the Son. He said that the Spirit had the same authority, power and glory as the Father and the Son.

Such is the case throughout the Bible. In the book of Acts, a man named Ananias, along with his wife, Sapphira, sold a possession and brought a certain part of the proceeds to the apostles, pretending that he had brought all. But the apostle Peter, filled with the Holy Spirit, rebuked Ananias: "Why hath Satan filled thine heart to lie to the Holy Ghost, and to keep back part of the price of the land?....Thou hast not lied unto men, but unto God" (Acts 5:3,4). Here Peter gave witness that the Holy Spirit is God by saying that Ananias had lied to God and the Holy Spirit, using the words interchangeably.

Some Old Testament verses spoken by the Lord are referred to in the New Testament as being written by the Holy Spirit. For example, Isaiah 6:9 says, "He [the Lord] said, Go, and tell this people, Hear ye indeed, but understand not; and see ye indeed, but perceive not." When Paul quoted this verse in the New Testament, he credited it to the Holy Spirit: "Well spake the Holy Ghost by Esaias the prophet unto our fathers, saying, Go unto this people, and say, Hearing ye shall hear, and shall not understand; and seeing ye shall see, and not perceive" (Acts 28:25,26).

From Scripture passages such as these I clearly understand that the Holy Spirit is indeed one of the holy trinity. The word of the Lord God of the Old Testament is the same as the word of the Holy Spirit in the New Testament (see also Jer. 31:33

and Heb. 10:15,16).

We can also see that the Holy Spirit is God in that He carries out the work that none but God can do. The Holy Spirit created the heavens and the earth by the will of God (see Gen. 1:2; Job 26:13). He raised the dead (see Rom. 1:4; 6:11); caused people to be born again (see John 3:5-7); reproved the world of sin, of righteousness and of judgment (see John 16:8); and cast out devils (see Matt. 12:28).

More than these proofs, the Holy Spirit has all the attributes of God. Only God is eternal, omniscient, omnipotent and omnipresent—and the Holy Spirit is all these.

Hebrews 9:14 says that the Holy Spirit is eternal: "How much more shall the blood of Christ, who through the eternal Spirit offered himself without spot to God, purge your conscience from dead works to serve the living God?"

The Holy Spirit is omniscient: "But God hath revealed them unto us by his Spirit: for the Spirit searcheth all things, yea, the deep things of God" (1 Cor. 2:10). The Holy Spirit knows *all* things, even the deep things of God.

The Holy Spirit is omnipotent: "And the angel answered and saith unto her [Mary], The Holy Ghost shall come upon thee, and the power of the Highest shall overshadow thee" (Luke 1:35). Clearly, the Holy Ghost is the power of the Highest, and nothing is impossible with God.

Finally, the Holy Spirit is omnipresent. Psalm 139 expresses well the omnipresence of the Holy Spirit. Speaking to the Lord, David says, "Whither shall I go from thy spirit? or whither shall I flee from thy presence? If I ascend up into heaven, thou art there: if I make my bed in hell, behold, thou art there" (vv. 7,8).

So isn't the Holy Spirit—who is eternal, omniscient, omnipotent and omnipresent—God? The Spirit is also majestic and holy and glorious, as is the Father and the Son.

The Holy Spirit Has a Personality

As soon as we realize that the Holy Spirit is a person—an entity who has a personality, as does the Father and the Son—our postures toward the Holy Spirit completely change. There are several ways the personal nature of the Holy Spirit affects our relationship to Him. In *The Person and Work of the Holy Spirit*, evangelist and Bible scholar R.A. Torrey pointed out the importance of the Holy Spirit's personality. He emphasized that only a being with a personality can understand our problems and give us help.

We cannot have dialogue with stones, trees or an impersonal force. But being a divine person, the Holy Spirit can deeply understand our affairs and help us. This allows us to seek His help.

The Korean hymnal includes several hymns of prayer to the Holy Spirit asking for His help. The first line of one such hymn petitions, "Spirit of the living God, fall afresh on me."

What a fervent prayer and song of supplication to the Holy Spirit! Besides this, there are hymns titled "Holy Ghost, the Infinite," "Gracious Spirit," "Come, Gracious Spirit," "Holy Ghost, With Light Divine," "Holy Spirit, Faithful Guide," all praying to the Holy Spirit. If the Holy Spirit were not a person, how could He know our circumstances and help us? Our hymns of prayer to the Holy Spirit would be foolish.

Biblical Evidence

You might ask how we know that the Holy Spirit is a person. This is made clear throughout the Bible.

People often do not distinguish between personality and

corporeality. When we say that any entity is a person, some falsely understand this to mean that this entity must have a fleshly form. But Jesus did not have a fleshly form like ours after He had been resurrected. As the apostle Paul said, "Though we have known Christ after the flesh, yet now henceforth know we him no more" (2 Cor. 5:16), for Jesus now has a spiritual body (see 1 Cor. 15:44). Does this mean that Jesus lost His personality? Of course not.

I don't know any believers who would disagree with the statement that the Father is a living person—yet no one has ever seen God, for God is a Spirit (see John 4:24). An entity is a person regardless of its corporeality, if it has the attributes of a person. Since the Holy Spirit has all the attributes of a person, even though He is not visible, He is a person. Let's look at the biblical proofs of this.

We know the Holy Spirit is a person because the Bible continually uses personal pronouns to refer to the Holy Spirit. "Even the Spirit of truth, which proceedeth from the Father, he shall testify of me" (John 15:26). "If I go not away, the Comforter will not come unto you; but if I depart, I will send him unto you....And when he is come, he will reprove the world of sin, and of righteousness, and of judgment" (John 16:7,8). "Howbeit when he, the Spirit of truth, is come, he will guide you into all truth" (John 16:13).

Many acts that only a person can perform are ascribed to the Holy Spirit. Here is a brief list of these personal actions:

1. The Holy Spirit *speaks*: "He that hath an ear, let him hear what the Spirit saith unto the churches" (Rev. 2:7).

2. The Holy Spirit *helps us in our weakness*: "Likewise the Spirit also helpeth our infirmities" (Rom. 8:26).

3. The Holy Spirit *prays for us*: "The Spirit itself maketh intercession for us" (Rom. 8:26).

4. The Holy Spirit *teaches us*: "But the Comforter, which is the Holy Ghost, whom the Father will send in my name, he shall teach you all things, and bring all things to your remembrance, whatsoever I have said unto you" (John 14:26).

5. The Holy Spirit *testifies of the Lord*: "But when the Comforter is come...he shall testify of me" (John 15:26).

6. The Holy Spirit *guides us*: "Howbeit when he, the Spirit of truth, is come, he will guide you into all truth" (John 16:13).

7. The Holy Spirit *commands people* in their service of Jesus Christ: "Now when they...were forbidden of the Holy Ghost to preach the word in Asia...they assayed to go into Bithynia, but the Spirit suffered them not" (Acts 16:6,7).

8. The Holy Spirit *calls people* to the work of God and appoints them to office: "The Holy Ghost said, Separate me Barnabas and Saul for the work whereunto I have called them" (Acts 13:2).

9. The Holy Spirit *comforts believers*: "Then had the churches rest...and were edified; and walking in the fear of the Lord, and in the comfort of the Holy Ghost, were multiplied" (Acts 9:31).

Actually, whole chapters of the Bible were written about the activities of the Holy Spirit. This list gives only some highlights.

Characteristics of personality are ascribed to the Holy Spirit. To be a person, an entity must have certain attributes: the knowledge of things and facts; feelings such as joy, anger, pleasure and sorrow; and the will to decide one's attitudes toward these feelings. Does the Holy Spirit have all these attributes?

First, knowledge is ascribed to the Holy Spirit, as shown in these passages: "But God hath revealed them unto us by his Spirit: for the Spirit searcheth all things, yea, the deep things of God" (1 Cor. 2:10); "He that searcheth the hearts knoweth what is the mind of the Spirit'' (Rom. 8:27).

Think about it. The Holy Spirit has the intellect to search the deep things of God as well as He searches and understands the human heart.

Let me tell you about my own experience concerning the knowledge of the Holy Spirit. On one sultry summer day, I preached to about 1,300 people attending an evening service at my church. About halfway through my sermon, I suddenly was impressed in my spirit by an irresistible prompting of the Holy Spirit. He revealed to me that a person in the congregation had left home to commit suicide and if that individual was not saved tonight, that was the end of the line. After receiving that knowledge, I tried to continue my sermon as if nothing had happened. But I felt too constrained. I finally stopped the sermon for a few minutes and explained the situation to the congregation. "If such a person is present," I asked, "please raise your hand."

A young woman did raise her hand, and after the service, I met her at my office. Though she had left her home with the intention of never returning, she had been persuaded by a friend to come to the service. She had nothing in her mind but suicide until she had heard that God was interested in her and wanted to pull her out of her despair.

As we talked, she wept bitterly; she confessed her sins and returned home, saved. A year or so later I received a letter from her saying that she was leading a happy life in the Lord. An experience like that assures me that the Holy Spirit knows all our inner thoughts and our circumstances. Yes, the Holy Spirit has knowledge.

Second, the Holy Spirit has emotions and feelings, as noted in these passages: "And hope maketh not ashamed; because the love of God is shed abroad in our hearts by the Holy Ghost which is given unto us'' (Rom. 5:5); ''And grieve not the holy Spirit of God'' (Eph. 4:30); ''The Spirit itself maketh intercession for us with groanings which cannot be uttered'' (Rom. 8:26).

Such biblical passages prove that the Holy Spirit possesses a variety of emotions: He pours the love of God into our spirits, He can be grieved and He groans in earnest prayer in our behalf.

Third, the Holy Spirit has a will, and He works according to His will and plan. ''But all things worketh that one and the selfsame Spirit, dividing to every man severally as he will'' (1 Cor. 12:11). ''Now when they...were forbidden of the Holy Ghost to preach the word in Asia...they assayed to go into Bithynia: but the Spirit suffered them not'' (Acts 16:6,7).

One of the most foolish things people try to do today is use the Holy Spirit for their own purposes. The Holy Spirit is not an impersonal entity, some inanimate object or an unknown power to be used. He is a real person, and He uses people for His own work according to His will. In the summer of 1964, I keenly experienced this fact.

I had been in California for one week, preaching in several churches. I had just purchased my plane ticket to the state of Washington, when I suddenly felt very uneasy and troubled in my spirit. I tried to calm myself but I couldn't. I had planned to attend a party given by the Women's Missionary Council before I left town, and after arriving at the party, I asked the president of the women's meeting for a quiet place to pray. I knelt down before the Lord, and immediately the Holy Spirit clearly showed me that it was His will for me to remain in that city a week longer. For a while I enumerated my excuses— why I should leave—but I had no peace. Finally, when I submitted to the Lord and told Him I would obey Him, peace returned and flooded my heart and mind.

Reflecting back on that situation, I found that my obedience to the voice of the Lord brought good evangelistic results and fruit for the kingdom of God.

From personal experience I can tell you that the Holy Spirit has a will and a way to make that will known.

Beyond question, the Bible shows that the Holy Spirit is a real person who has knowledge, feeling and will. He abides and works with and within us. Knowing this, we should expedite our evangelism through His supernatural power by acknowledging, welcoming and worshipping Him in our personal walks and in our public ministries.

The Holy Spirit's personal nature is the reason our worship of Him is so important. Would we be required to worship an impersonal power? No. But praise His holy name He responds as a personality—perfect as He is God.

3

Names and Symbols of the Holy Spirit

The Bible uses at least four significant names in speaking of the Holy Spirit: *the Holy Spirit* (sometimes translated as the Holy Ghost), *the Spirit of God*, *the Spirit of Christ* and *the Comforter*. Each name has to do with a particular office of the Holy Spirit. Let's look at the names more closely and then go on to discuss the symbols used to describe Him.

The Holy Spirit

''God hath not called us unto uncleanness, but unto holiness. He therefore that despiseth, despiseth not man, but God, who hath also given unto us his holy Spirit'' (1 Thess. 4:7,8).

Among the three members of the holy trinity, the Holy Spirit particularly has the office of holiness and purity, as His name signifies. The Holy Spirit is the power that brings holiness and purity to believers. He sets them apart from the wickedness of this world, in which evil and unclean spirits work in the children of disobedience. It's by the Spirit of holiness that we can distinguish the spirit that belongs to God from the spirit that belongs to Satan.

The Spirit of God

"Grieve not the holy Spirit of God, whereby ye were sealed unto the day of redemption" (Eph. 4:30).

In many biblical passages the Holy Spirit is called the Spirit of God (see Gen. 1:2; 1 Cor. 2:11). It is appropriate that the Holy Spirit be called the Spirit of God, as the Spirit is sent by God (see John 15:26). The Bible also calls the Holy Spirit the Spirit of God because God works through the Holy Spirit, calling sinners to Jesus the Savior (see John 6:44), revealing the truth (see Matt. 11:25) and leading believers (see Rom. 8:14).

The Spirit of Christ

"Now if any man have not the Spirit of Christ, he is none of his" (Rom. 8:9).

The Holy Spirit is called the Spirit of Christ, because Jesus shed upon believers Him whom He had received of the Father (see Acts 2:33). Time and time again Jesus said that the Holy Spirit would come in His place and continue His work. He said that the coming of the Holy Spirit to dwell in the hearts of believers would be the coming of Christ Himself (see John 14:16-20). And He said that the Spirit would testify of Jesus' redeeming crucifixion and resurrection (see John 15:26).

Some people teach that the Holy Spirit is different from the Spirit of Christ, that one receives the Spirit of Christ when one is born again and the Holy Spirit when baptized by the Holy Spirit. If this is true, should we not pray to receive also the Spirit of the Father? This teaching is not based on the true knowledge of the holy trinity, but on false theology. The Spirit of Christ is the same as the Holy Spirit.

The Comforter

"But when the Comforter is come, whom I will send unto you from the Father, even the Spirit of truth, which proceedeth from the Father, he shall testify of me" (John 15:26). Jesus called the Holy Spirit "the Comforter," a name of endless mercy.

Paraclete, or "Comforter," has its root in two Greek words that mean "at one's side" and "to call." Etymologically this word originated from a court trial. When a defendant was pressed hard by a prosecutor and didn't know how to plead for himself, he looked around, hoping to find someone to help him. Seeing the familiar face of an influential friend, the defendant would beckon to him and the friend would make his way through the crowd to the defendant's side. From that moment, the friend stood by the defendant as his paraclete and helped him to win his case.

The Comforter is the one who gives solace and is called to stand by the side of a person in difficulty. He counsels, pleads, entreats, exhorts and strengthens so that a person can gain victory over his opponents.

Let's think more deeply about the words of Jesus: "I will pray the Father, and he shall give you another Comforter, that he may abide with you for ever" (John 14:16).

It seems evident that Jesus considered Himself the first Comforter, because He describes the Holy Spirit, who would take His place and work in His name, as "another" Comforter.

The latter half of 1 John 2:1 reads: "If any man sin, we have an advocate with the Father, Jesus Christ the righteous.'' The Greek word translated ''advocate'' here is *parakletos*, the same word translated ''Comforter'' in John 14:16 and 26. This again shows Jesus as the first Comforter (the Holy Spirit being another Comforter).

The adjective ''another'' in John 14:16 has significant implications in the original Greek. Two different Greek words are used in the Bible to denote ''another.'' The first one is found in John 14:16, ''another Comforter''; the second is found in Galatians 1:6, ''another gospel.'' The ''another'' of John 14:16 is the Greek word *allos*, which signifies another of the same kind and quality. The word ''another'' of Galatians 1:6 is the Greek word *heteros*, which denotes another which is different in kind and quality.

Surprisingly, when Jesus referred to ''another Comforter,'' He used the words *allos parakletos*. Why? Because, although the Holy Spirit is a different person from Jesus, He is the same kind of Comforter, of the same divine nature and with the same purpose as Jesus. He glorifies the name of Jesus, instead of Himself, and works in the place of Jesus. Therefore, the indwelling of our Comforter, the Holy Spirit, is analogous to the same presence of Jesus. When Jesus told about the coming of the Holy Spirit, He said it was like the coming of Jesus Himself: ''I will not leave you comfortless: I will come to you'' (John 14:18). The abiding of the Holy Spirit is the abiding of Jesus, and the fullness of the Holy Spirit is the fullness of Jesus. Such a wonderful blessing is a supernatural and miraculous experience, quite beyond our description.

Water

The Bible is full of symbols that refer to the Holy Spirit. Now that we've looked at who He is and what He is named, we can also study the properties of the metaphors used to describe Him. Let's start with *water*.

"Jesus stood and cried, saying, If any man thirst, let him come unto me, and drink. He that believeth on me, as the scripture hath said, out of his belly shall flow rivers of living water" (John 7:37,38).

In many places in the Bible water is used as a symbol of the Holy Spirit. Why is this an apt metaphor? By observing the relationship between water and human life we can understand a great deal about the Holy Spirit.

First, water is indispensable to the preservation of life. A human being is composed of sixty percent water. If dehydrated by much vomiting or diarrhea, a person is in danger of losing physical life. Similarly, the Holy Spirit is indispensable to our spiritual life. We are born again of the Holy Spirit (see John 3:5), and by continuously drinking of the Holy Spirit (see 1 Cor. 12:13), we can preserve our spiritual life. Through the Holy Spirit we become energetic, enjoying the satisfying life in which we shall never thirst (see John 4:13,14).

Water is also indispensable to the cleansing of our bodies. If we had no access to water for a long time, wouldn't the filthiness and corruption eventually make us sick, even to death? Every day we wash our bodies, our clothes, our kitchen counters. So our spiritual lives should be cleansed daily by the Holy Spirit. Of course, we are cleansed from our sins when we believe in the precious blood of Jesus; but the Holy Spirit—as if washing us with water—refreshes us, renewing our hearts so we can lead clean lives (see Titus 3:5).

The Holy Spirit is the origin of life to those who are obedient, but He is the Spirit of judgment, a consuming flood, to those who are disobedient. In the days of Noah, God judged the world by the flood for the sins and disobedience of the people (see Gen. 7). God judged Pharaoh and his army, destroying them in the Red Sea (see Ex. 14:28). In Acts 5, Ananias and Sapphira died by the judgment of the Holy Spirit, whom they lied against. Acts 13 tells the story of Elymas, a sorcerer who became blind by the judgment of the Holy Spirit when he opposed Paul's preaching of the gospel.

Fire

"He [Jesus] shall baptize you with the Holy Ghost, and with fire" (Matt. 3:11).

Fire is a popular symbol of the Holy Spirit, but the truth the metaphor implies is not so well known. First, fire was used as the symbol of the Holy Spirit because throughout the Old Testament, without exception, the presence of God appeared in fire. Some wonderful historic events show that fire accompanies the presence of God. In the days when Moses kept his father-in-law's flock on Mount Horeb, Moses met with God when he was looking at a flaming bush (see Ex. 3:1-5).

In 1 Kings 18 when Elijah contended with the 450 prophets of Baal on Mount Carmel, he insisted that He who answered by fire before all the people would be God! When Elijah actually received the answer by fire, he destroyed the idolators.

After the ascension of Jesus, 120 disciples gathered together in an upper room in Jerusalem. They were encouraging one another amidst much despair and waiting for the promise of the Lord, the Holy Spirit. Then, on the feast of Pentecost: "Suddenly there came a sound from heaven as of a rushing mighty wind, and it filled all the house where they were sitting. And there appeared unto them cloven tongues like as of fire, and it sat upon each of them" (Acts 2:2,3).

Here we can see that the Holy Spirit, whom Jesus sent, also appeared in the midst of fire. It is apparent that God works in the flame of the Holy Spirit.

Second, fire burns away that which is unwanted. The most perfect method of purification known to mankind is by fire: All kinds of filthy and ugly things are burned off.

As the Holy Spirit dwells within our lives, He consumes sin in us (see Heb. 12:29; Jer. 23:29). Holy and righteous living is not possible unless this consuming work takes place within our hearts.

Third, fire provides us with light which enlarges the sphere and hours of our activity. Human civilization is called the civilization of light. If it were possible to sustain life without the light of the sun, can you imagine how furiously people would resist the lack? How diligently people seek the fire that illumines the physical world, while being indifferent to the fire of the Holy Spirit that brightens the eternal soul. The Holy Spirit comes into our hearts, pitch dark with sin and death, and by shedding His divine light of heaven, He helps us realize eternal life and see the secret of heaven.

Fourth, the Holy Spirit is symbolized by fire because fire gives us supernatural zeal. When the Holy Spirit gets hold of our hearts, a love of the Lord and an enthusiasm for the work of the gospel flames like fire within our spirits.

Fifth, fire symbolizes power. The machine power that drives our civilization is obtained primarily by means of combustion. Supersonic jet planes, trucks, trains—all provide convenience for us through the power of a spark, a fire.

Thus the Holy Spirit provides us with the power of heaven, urgently needed for our personal lives of faith and for the ministry of gospel preaching. It is reckless to try to start the work of the gospel without receiving the divine power provided by the fire of the Holy Spirit.

THE HOLY SPIRIT, MY SENIOR PARTNER

Wind

"The wind bloweth where it listeth, and thou hearest the sound thereof, but canst not tell whence it cometh, and whither it goeth: so is every one that is born of the Spirit" (John 3:8).

The Greek word for wind and spirit is the same—*pneuma*. Therefore, literally translated, the Holy Spirit is the "Holy Wind." There is so much grace in this metaphor of the Holy Spirit. Why do I say that?

First, the wind exists pervasively everywhere on the earth. The air we breathe is there in every empty vessel or in every place, however small it may be. Jesus said that the Holy Spirit would be with us forever; there is no place on the earth where the Holy Spirit is not present. He works all around the earth so that no one can either monopolize or resist Him. As explained in the Bible, we are not deserted like orphans when we acknowledge, welcome, invite and depend upon the Holy Spirit (see John 14:18).

Second, the wind is air in continuous motion. We feel the wind moving when the air flows from high atmospheric pressure to low atmospheric pressure in accordance with weather patterns. So the Holy Spirit is also continually working. It is not true that the Holy Spirit worked in the days of the Old Testament and the early days of the New Testament, and then vanished like a mist. Just as the wind blows today as it did centuries ago, so the Holy Spirit works continuously.

The Holy Spirit flows into areas of low atmospheric pressure—sin, sickness, sorrow and despair—and is ever ready to work with the joyful message of forgiveness, healing and eternal life. As many as come to the Lord with penitent and obedient hearts will experience the regenerating work of the Holy Spirit.

Third, we cannot control the direction of the wind as we wish.

Jesus said that the wind blows as it will (see John 3:8). Since the Holy Spirit has the supreme will and works according to His own purpose, we should follow the direction of the Holy Spirit obediently, as we walk by faith.

Fourth, a blowing wind makes stifling and stagnant air fresh and full of vitality. What wonderful relief the fresh wind gives on a stifling and sultry summer day! The wind blowing into a room full of toxic gas makes the entire atmosphere refreshed and pure.

So it is with the working of the Holy Spirit. When we become depressed and lifeless with the anxieties of living and the temptations of sin, the Holy Spirit comes into our hearts like wind with the new life and vitality of heaven. By pouring it out upon our spirits, He makes us full of the joy of life and the zeal of faith.

Oil

"Then Samuel took the horn of oil, and anointed him in the midst of his brethren: and the Spirit of the Lord came upon David from that day forward" (1 Sam. 16:13). "The anointing which ye have received of him abideth in you" (1 John 2:27).

Throughout the Old and New Testaments the Holy Spirit is symbolized by oil. Again, this symbol can teach us the work of the Holy Spirit.

First, anointed places and persons are holy, set apart unto God. God commanded Moses to sanctify the tabernacle of the congregation, the ark of the testimony, all the instruments and the altar by anointing them with oil (see Ex. 30:25-29). Moses also anointed Aaron and his sons, consecrating them that they might minister unto God in the priest's office (see Ex. 30:30). God told Samuel to anoint David as king (see 1 Sam. 16:13), and Elijah anointed Elisha to be prophet (see 1 Kin. 19:16).

Today God makes those who believe in the Lord Jesus Christ a chosen generation, a royal priesthood, a holy nation and a peculiar people by the anointing of the Holy Spirit (see 1 Pet. 2:9). No one can receive such grace without being empowered by the Holy Spirit.

We are born again of the Holy Spirit and we have obtained the office of prophet whereby we preach the Word. We shall one day reign with Christ anointed by the Holy Spirit. How can we help but thank God?

Second, oil was necessary to light the seven candlesticks in the tabernacle of God. In the sanctuary of the Old Testament, the only light came from the golden candlesticks—and the oil. Likewise, only through the bright light of the anointing Holy Spirit can the spiritual world be revealed to us.

Just as no other light was permitted to light the holy place, in the same way, only the light from the oil of the Holy Spirit can illumine the Word of God—the secret of heaven's holy place.

Third, oil prevents wear and tear and breakdown by relieving the friction between moving parts. How could we lubricate the human spirit, strained and torn with endless discord? Why have even churches and Christians been so disruptive? Because we have not been anointed by the Holy Spirit. The lubricating oil of peace, love and healing comes only when we are filled with the Holy Spirit.

Fourth, oil is a necessary ingredient for the preservation of life. Why have the spirits of some believers become dried up like the bones in the valley of Ezekiel's vision? Why has the church become so emaciated in quality as well as quantity?

Because they have not received the oil of the Holy Spirit, the heavenly nutrition indispensable to our spirits. History and reality prove clearly that churches, as well as individual Christians, which are full of the Holy Spirit are well-nourished. It was so in the past and it will always be so.

Rain

"He shall come down like rain upon the mown grass: as showers that water the earth" (Ps. 72:6). "Then shall we know, if we follow on to know the Lord: his going forth is prepared as the morning; and he shall come unto us as the rain, as the latter and former rain unto the earth" (Hos. 6:3).

There are two clear reasons for the metaphor of the Holy Spirit as rain. Think about the earth: It can neither bear any fruit nor sustain any kind of life unless it receives rain. In the lifetime of the Old Testament prophet Elijah, when all the herbs and trees were scorched and vegetation died, Elijah prayed earnestly that it might rain. It did and the earth brought forth fruit. Thus, as the earth can bear fruit and preserve life only when it receives rain, so a person's spiritual life can revive, to bear spiritual fruit and preserve powerful spiritual life, only when it receives the rain of the Holy Spirit.

A second reason the Holy Spirit is symbolized as rain watering the earth is a little more complex. In Palestine farmers expect rain twice during each growing season. The first rain falls in late autumn and is called the "early rain." When the early rain comes, the farmers quickly sow their wheat or barley seed which absorbs the moisture of that rain. The seed sprouts and comes up, but during the cold winter it barely stays alive. When springtime returns, warm winds from the southeast blow and the rain falls again, giving new life. The Palestinian farmers call this springtime rain the "latter rain." And after the plants absorb this, the crops grow rapidly until harvest.

This natural cycle is mentioned in relation to the Holy Spirit in the book of James. "Be patient therefore, brethren, unto the coming of the Lord. Behold, the husbandman waiteth for the precious fruit of the earth, and hath long patience for it, until he receive the early and latter rain" (5:7).

When the Lord Jesus came to earth, He sowed the seed of the gospel. Ten days after His ascension, on the day of Pentecost, 120 believers who had received this seed gathered together in Jerusalem. When they were praying, a sound from heaven like that of a rushing mighty wind filled the house where they were gathered. Cloven tongues of fire sat upon each of them and they were filled with the Holy Ghost. At that moment the church of Jesus Christ came into being. This "early rain" of the Holy Spirit was then poured out in Samaria and in a worship service at the home of Cornelius and on the believers in Ephesus. With the life and power of the Spirit, churches of Jesus Christ were built in place after place, and the Word of life came to be preached vigorously. This work of the Holy Spirit, the early rain, was poured out abundantly until A.D. 300. It then started to diminish and around A.D. 600 the work of the Holy Spirit almost ceased. The church became ritualistic, and the hard winter of faith approached. The church went through the dark ages.

During the Reformation in the sixteenth century, through the efforts of men like Martin Luther, the work of the Holy Spirit revived. Thereafter, through faithful servants of the Lord such as John Wesley, George Whitefield, Charles Finney and Dwight Moody, the great work of the Holy Spirit reappeared. Around the year 1900 the whole world began once again to receive the Holy Spirit.

Now that the church has received the Holy Spirit in the abundant "latter rain," we are witnessing the work of the Holy Spirit as did the early church. Though some people don't understand the work of God in this present time and oppose this move of the Holy Spirit, no one can resist the work and will of God; His work will be accomplished without fail. We cannot but give thanks, praise and honor to God who restores to us the power of the early church by pouring out the latter rain of the Holy Spirit.

When I was invited to attend the Eighth World Pentecostal Conference held in Rio de Janeiro, Brazil, I could not help admiring the wonderful work of the Holy Spirit. In that Catholic country rooted in ceremonies and rituals, as many as three million people were said to have received the Holy Spirit according to Acts 2:4.

Now, before the second coming of the Lord Jesus, the Holy Spirit is once again awakening the church around the world and pouring out His grace—setting souls free through belief in Jesus Christ. Realizing that now is the opportune time to revitalize our faith by receiving the latter rain of the Spirit, we should pray fervently.

Dove

"And John bare record, saying, I saw the Spirit descending from heaven like a dove, and it abode upon him" (John 1:32).

This verse describes the most prominent occasion when the Holy Spirit was symbolized as a dove: when Jesus was baptized by John the Baptist in the Jordan River. When the heavens were opened, the Spirit of God descended like a dove and lighted upon Jesus. There are deep meanings in the metaphor of a dove symbolizing the Holy Spirit.

First, all over the world the dove is known as an emblem of peace. In Genesis, when God destroyed all flesh by the deluge, Noah and the seven members of his family found grace in the eyes of God. They were saved in the ark. Forty days after the ark rested on Mount Ararat, Noah released a dove through the window of the ark to see if the waters had abated. The dove returned, and Genesis 8 relates: "And he [Noah] stayed yet other seven days; and again he sent forth the dove out of the ark; and the dove came in to him in the evening; and, lo, in her mouth was an olive leaf plucked off: so Noah knew that the waters were abated from off the earth" (vv. 10,11).

The first evidence to show that peace had returned on the earth and that the judgment and wrath of God had passed away was a dove.

How beautifully this signifies the presence of the Holy Spirit, who never comes to human spirits that are under the judgment and wrath of God. Jesus Christ redeemed us by His death on the cross, thereby paying for the wrath and judgment of God. When we confess our sins and accept Jesus as our Savior, the Holy Spirit comes to us because we have the redeeming proof of the precious blood. The Holy Spirit makes us feel the joy of knowing that we "shall not come into condemnation; but... passed from death unto life" (John 5:24) and "have peace with God" (Rom. 5:1).

And this is not all! To those who in their sin walk toward hell, opposing and disobeying God, the Holy Spirit keeps preaching the reconciling gospel of peace. The most important thing anyone must decide today is whether to receive salvation and peace—the joyful news the Holy Spirit brings into our hearts—or be destroyed.

The dove is also a symbol of meekness and humility— attributes of the Holy Spirit that He imparts to us. It always puzzles me to see people who profess to having received the Holy Spirit act and speak insultingly. Some behave as if they have been taken by a spirit of evil. But the evidence of the

Holy Spirit is a meek and humble spirit.

The dove is also known as a pure and harmless creature. The dove does not kill other animals like the cat or eagle. In a corresponding vein, note that the Holy Spirit is a *holy* Spirit.

Close relatives of those who are stricken by evil spirits frequently bring their family members to my office, asking me to discern the spiritual state of their loved ones. As I talk with these suffering people, they confess without exception that lewdness, wrong thinking and abusive language flow through them against their own wills. These are the works of the devil. Such people should determine to stand firmly on the Word of truth and continuously fight against Satan until they drive him out, relying upon the cleansing power of the precious blood of Jesus. If they don't, they will surely become mentally disabled in the end. Fortunately, I can say to those who worry about this that they can be set perfectly free by the precious blood of the Lamb and the power of God's Word.

The Holy Spirit is always a *holy* Spirit. Because there can be no ugliness in Him, we should never allow any spiritual change in us that is not toward holiness. Of course, we do not become holy instantly when we receive the Holy Spirit. Through receiving the Holy Spirit we receive power to grow holy and we receive a sensitivity that makes us feel guilty when we commit sin. If we heed this, our lives cannot help but become better.

The Holy Spirit has not come to bite, tear and kill but to save, heal and bind up. Carefully note Jesus' proclamation at the synagogue of Nazareth concerning what He would do by the help of the Holy Spirit: "The Spirit of the Lord is upon me, because he hath anointed me to preach the gospel to the poor; he hath sent me to heal the brokenhearted, to preach deliverance to the captives, and recovering of sight to the blind, to set at liberty them that are bruised, to preach the acceptable year of the Lord'' (Luke 4:18,19).

The fourth reason the Holy Spirit is symbolized as a dove is that the Holy Spirit is easily grieved: the works of the Holy Spirit are quenched by the betrayal of mankind. More than any other animal, the dove is easily frightened. Harassed once or twice, a dove will leave that place forever. To live in harmony with the Holy Spirit in our hearts, we must be very careful to have a reverent attitude toward Him and not grieve Him. Ephesians 4:30 warns us: ''Grieve not the holy Spirit of God.'' If we continually oppose the Holy Spirit, He will leave us like a dove—what a terrible and fearful thing. When repenting, David prayed earnestly, weeping before God after he had sinned: ''Cast me not away from thy presence; and take not thy holy spirit from me'' (Ps. 51:11).

The Holy Spirit that descended in the form of a beautiful dove and lighted upon Jesus comes down upon us today eager to fill our hearts.

Wine

''And be not drunk with wine, wherein is excess; but be filled with the Spirit'' (Eph. 5:18). ''And they were all amazed, and were in doubt saying one to another, what meaneth this? Others mocking said, These men are full of new wine'' (Acts 2:12,13).

The Bible contrasts, or in some cases compares, the fullness of the Holy Spirit with drunkenness. Those who have experienced the fullness of the Holy Spirit will well understand what this means.

Like wine, the fullness of the Holy Spirit gives gladness and joy to our hearts. But, though the result of drinking wine is physical harm and dissipation, the fullness of the Holy Spirit brings spiritual joy and the eventual pleasure of heaven. The Spirit-filled life has wonderfully beneficial results: ''Speaking to yourselves in psalms and hymns and spiritual songs, singing and making melody in your hearts to the Lord; giving thanks always for all things unto God and the Father in the name of our Lord Jesus Christ; submitting yourselves one to another in the fear of God'' (Eph. 5:19-21). The fullness of the Spirit also makes us strong in faith and helps us serve God—not with temporary excitement but with continuous enjoyment.

Wine makes people seem merry and it also gives temporary peace of mind. It makes one forget anxiety, care and sorrow. But such a state is not normal, but intoxication. The wine that is the Holy Spirit does not anesthetize; it brings about the most normal state of overflowing peace, allowing us to set aside worldly anxieties, cares and worries as our Creator intended.

A third effect of wine is that it gives unusual boldness that causes people to take arrogant, wild, unrestrained actions. Life filled with the Holy Spirit is also a bold life. The Holy Spirit can change even a timid and shy person into one who is not afraid to give up life itself. The boldness that comes with the fullness of the Holy Spirit enables us to love truth and justice, to be meek and humble, to preach the gospel with authority. The fullness of the Holy Spirit makes us bold to conquer sin and live a victorious life.

Finally, drunken people often do not feel physical pain because the senses have been anesthetized. I once saw a dead-drunk foreign soldier clutching a wire entanglement. He wasn't even aware that his hands were bloody from handling the tearing barbed wires. The Holy Spirit does not dull physical senses, but the power of His love and His strength to persevere can insulate us from personal and spiritual blows. The Holy Spirit gives us the strength to stand firm.

It is true that those who are filled with the Holy Spirit often resemble drunken people. But intoxication with wine is a harmful excess while the fullness of the Holy Spirit makes one perfect.

Seal

"[Christ] in whom ye also trusted, after that ye heard the word of truth, the gospel of your salvation: in whom also after that ye believed, ye were sealed with that holy Spirit of promise" (Eph. 1:13).

How wonderful that receiving the Holy Spirit is compared to being sealed, for that is how we come to possess the assurance of our salvation. Let's consider for a moment the symbolic meaning in the metaphor of sealing.

First, sealing means to stamp something to guard against its being opened by an unauthorized person. In other words, if something is sealed, no one may touch it without permission. When Pilate sealed the stone that enclosed Jesus' grave, removal of the stone without Pilate's permission was punishable by death. Thus, if we are sealed by the blood of Jesus, God keeps us from falling into sin by the power of the Holy Spirit.

Therefore, we believers—sealed by the Holy Spirit and relying upon His power—should sanctify our minds and lives, so as to defeat sin and the devil.

Second, sealing signifies special ownership—which we experience daily. Think of it this way: No one can draw my money out of the bank without my seal or signature. If I stamp my possessions with my seal, everyone knows that those valuables are mine. Anyone who tried to disregard the seal and take them would infringe on my rights of ownership and legally incur serious consequences.

Likewise, God proves that His people are indeed His by sealing them with the Holy Spirit. If anyone dares oppose or injure the anointed people of God, that person infringes on the ownership of God and brings God's wrath upon himself. When those people who have been sealed by the Holy Spirit humble themselves, obey the will of God and live for His glory, then the Lord of heaven and earth will be their protector and shelter.

Third, sealing signifies authority. Here in Korea everyone must have a certificate of residence. If it weren't stamped with an official seal, it would be good for nothing: it would have no authority.

Believers, as children of God, have authority. While the disciples were with Jesus, they worked many signs and wonders, and acted with authority and power. But after Jesus ascended into heaven they were defeated and miserably incompetent—until they were filled with the Holy Spirit. Then they suddenly had great authority in words. Power followed their words and prayer, giving them courage and boldness. As a result of their own God-given authority, their belief in God's full authority mushroomed.

Guarantee

"Now he which stablisheth us with you in Christ, and hath anointed us, is God: Who hath also sealed us, and given the earnest of the Spirit in our hearts" (2 Cor. 1:21,22).

Let us understand the wonderful blessing of the Holy Spirit by looking into the full meaning of a guarantee, which is what is meant by the word "earnest."

First, think of the most ordinary and common guarantee situations. For example, a person who becomes surety makes himself responsible for the conduct or debts of the one he guarantees. The responsibility of a guarantor is serious business.

We can firmly believe that we are saved, yet Satan endlessly shoots arrows of apprehension and doubt at our hearts. He deceives us with many subtle lies: "Do you think that heaven really exists? Forget such foolish thoughts! To have faith is to have religion, and as for religion, it makes no difference which one you have, as all religions are the same!''

At such a time, if it were not for the Holy Spirit who guarantees the validity of the gospel of Jesus, our spirits would go down; in the end we would fail, without faith. But when we are filled with the Holy Spirit—and the Holy Spirit continuously guarantees and assures the truthfulness of the Word—all the arrows of Satan are finally stopped. Thus, the Holy Spirit is with us as our surety, helping us believe without a doubt that God is real and that Jesus is our Savior. Hallelujah!

Second, when we buy goods at a store on the monthly installment plan, or sign a contract to purchase a house or a piece of land, we bind our agreement securely by paying earnest money in advance. If I fulfill my obligation in a certain period of time, I know I will eventually possess it and that the property will be mine.

Heaven is just like that. Our being saved by faith and receiving the Holy Spirit is our guarantee. While on this earth, by faith and obedience we should live fervently in accordance with God's Word, otherwise the earnest becomes void. We must be careful that we do not lose our precious deliverance by giving offense to God and falling into sin. If we walk in faith, being sober and vigilant, the Holy Spirit makes us overflow with joy and hope. His continued encouragement that heaven is ours is the earnest of the inheritance which will one day be our possession.

Third, a guarantee has an interesting symbolism in the traditional Middle Eastern bargaining process. When one contracted to purchase a piece of land from another, the buyer returned home with a large bag full of earth from the seller's land. He would place the earth in some corner of his house, and when he looked at it, smelled it and touched it, he had assurance that he had purchased the land. The bag of soil was his guarantee.

What is the spiritual parallel? The Holy Spirit is our guarantee of heaven. We have not yet gone there in person to possess and enjoy it, but we have been given a taste of it in the Holy Spirit.

What is heaven like? While we walk the paths of life, we do not live in mere endless imagination about heaven. Even now we possess part of heaven in our hearts. God permits us to enjoy in advance just a taste of the joy, peace and everlasting rest of heaven by sending the Holy Spirit to our spirits to satisfy those desires. What wonderful love this is!

By receiving this foretaste of heaven, we more earnestly long for heaven and therefore devote ourselves more fervently to the life of faith to obtain it.

4

Unbelievers and the Holy Spirit

The Bible describes the spiritual state of unbelievers as being "dead in trespasses and sins" (Eph. 2:1). This does not mean that unbelievers don't have souls. Rather, their souls are so far away from heaven and the life of God that they are insensitive to God and His kingdom. If they continue to remain in such a state, when they die physically their souls will fall into hell, which is completely separated from heaven and God.

How can we make such souls in a callous state—"dead in trespasses and sins"—realize their sins and accept the eternal life God gives? There is One who does such a work unceasingly among unbelievers—none other than the Holy Spirit. The Bible teaches: "Eye hath not seen, nor ear heard, neither have entered into the heart of man, the things which God hath prepared for them that love him. But God hath revealed them unto us by his Spirit'' (1 Cor. 2:9,10).

In other words, unbelievers cannot understand the salvation of God through their five senses or reason. Only through the power of inward revelation can they receive the light of understanding concerning salvation.

How does the Holy Spirit work when He approaches unbelievers? Concerning this, Jesus Himself gives a good explanation in John 16:8, when He says that the Holy Spirit ''will reprove the world of sin.''

Reproving the World of Sin

Every person has been born with a sinful nature. Psalm 51:5 reads, ''Behold, I was shapen in iniquity; and in sin did my mother conceive me.''

Someone may ask, ''What does that have to do with me?'' When we consider the original meaning of *sin*, we find that we are in a frightful position. We understand that it is impossible for us to contend that we have nothing to do with sin.

People usually call something a sin or unrighteousness when they see outward evidence of sin. But sin is rooted in deeper places than evidenced by specific trespasses. The Bible shows how and why man cannot help but bear sinful fruits.

A person's sinful state involves being separated from God. This sinful state, called original sin, is carried corporately: ''by one man sin entered into the world, and death by sin'' (Rom. 5:12); ''through the offence of one many be dead'' (Rom. 5:15).

Adam disobeyed God and was driven out from God's presence; in such a state, Adam produced mankind. As a result, all descendants of Adam—without having time to question it—are born in the state of being separated from God.

As a more familiar example, suppose a certain couple was

exiled to a lonely island and there the wife gave birth to children. The children could not determine their place of birth, far away from their homeland. Even if they chose to blame their father for their isolated circumstances of birth, their circumstances would not change. It's simply the way it happened.

Thus the descendants of Adam have been born in the sinful state of Adam—driven away from the presence of God and placed under Adam's sentence of death. The person who left the God of all righteousness, goodness and life cannot help but breed unrighteousness and trespasses. In this forsaken condition, mankind would die and go to hell. But here the great love and mercy of God appeared; God delivered us through our Lord, Jesus Christ.

Born of the virgin Mary, Jesus came into this world without original sin. He lived a life of no sin or guile. As a sinless person He became the perfect substitute for sinners. As a righteous person He was crucified for the unrighteous, and after three days He rose from the dead. By His death He paid the total price of our original sin and our self-committed sins. What does that mean? As many as believe in Him and receive the free grace of salvation receive eternal life. They are no longer separated from God.

Since Jesus' resurrection, man does not die eternally for his own sinful acts or for original sin. He is destroyed for not accepting the salvation of Jesus Christ. Because of this, I can't emphasize too much how urgently the gospel message should be preached.

How can we awaken the dead and senseless soul to receive this great gospel message? Who can convince sinners, who often do not realize their desperate state, of the danger to come and prompt them to flee to the shelter of salvation?

Men and women could never do these things. But God

promised to carry out this work by sending the Holy Spirit, who is performing this work all over the world through the church's proclamation of the gospel. We cannot but praise Him with all of our hearts.

Reproving the World of Righteousness

The Holy Spirit also "will reprove the world...of righteousness:...because I go to my Father, and ye see me no more" (John 16:8,10).

What is righteousness? When those who live outside the faith of Christ hear the word *righteousness*, they generally think of human behavior. When a person does something legally or morally unblamable, he or she is called righteous.

But what does God say to those who stand before the law of God? "All have sinned, and come short of the glory of God" (Rom. 3:23). "By the deeds of the law there shall no flesh be justified in his sight: for by the law is the knowledge of sin" (Rom. 3:20). Everyone who stands before the law of God is a sinner. Therefore, all not only come short of the glory of God, but they cannot help being driven out of His presence.

Then who can stand before the bright, glorious throne of God with a pure life totally free from sin? Being people who are descended from Adam, we are unable to find such a person— except for Jesus Christ, whom the Holy Spirit conceived in the virgin Mary and of whom He now bears witness. But what is the proof that this very Jesus lived a completely righteous life before God?

The evidence is clear. As previously noted, the apostle Paul said, "All have sinned, and come short of the glory of God." This means that sinners are not qualified to stand before God.

But remember, Jesus said that the Holy Spirit would convict the world of righteousness—"because I go to my Father, and ye see me no more'' (John 16:10).

Was such a claim of Jesus really accomplished? Yes. What He said would happen, did come to pass.

Jesus died by crucifixion, bearing all the sins of the world. He was buried, and His tomb was tightly secured by the hands of His enemies. In spite of that, He rose from the dead and later ascended into heaven in the presence of witnesses. His body was never discovered—though people looked for it.

As a surer evidence than this, fifty days after His death, Jesus sent the gift of the Holy Spirit to His disciples to enable them to see and hear clearly.

Peter said this about that experience: ''This Jesus hath God raised up, whereof we all are witnesses. Therefore being by the right hand of the Father exalted, and having received of the Father the promise of the Holy Ghost, he hath shed forth this, which ye now see and hear'' (Acts 2:32,33).

All flesh, whether saints or sinners, since the beginning of human history eventually died and left behind their physical remains (except Enoch and Elijah who were taken to heaven without seeing death, being counted righteous through their faith). But the empty grave of Jesus Christ silently witnesses that Jesus is alive, that He returned to His Father.

What does Jesus' righteousness mean to us? A sinner can never redeem another's sins. But Jesus' death did redeem our sins. Let me quote Romans 3:23 again—along with verse 24: ''All have sinned, and come short of the glory of God; being justified freely by his grace through the redemption that is in Christ Jesus.''

Also note these references to what was accomplished by Jesus' death and resurrection: ''He [God the Father] hath made him [Jesus] to be sin for us, who knew no sin; that we might be made the righteousness of God in him'' (2 Cor. 5:21); ''[Jesus]

71

was delivered for our offences, and was raised again for our justification" (Rom. 4:25). Jesus fully paid all the debts of mankind on the cross.

The Holy Spirit now bears witness that through faith in Jesus *anyone* can be counted as if he or she had never committed a sin. That means we can stand before the glory of God without a spot of shame, relying upon the merit of Jesus. What wonderful grace and tremendous blessing this is!

The Holy Spirit works unceasingly to convince the world of such wonderful truth and grace so that everyone may believe in the Savior, Jesus Christ, and be saved from the eternal destruction that comes apart from Christ. Today there is no flesh who can be justified by his or her own works before God, but through the grace of redemption in Christ the abundant gift of justification and entrance into the glorious kingdom of God is available to anyone.

Reproving the World of Judgment

Jesus also said the Holy Spirit would "reprove the world...of judgment:...because the prince of this world is judged" (John 16:8,11). What is this *judgment* that the Bible speaks of? And who is "the prince of this world"? Revelation 12:9-11 reads:

> And the great dragon was cast out, that old serpent, called the Devil, and Satan, which deceiveth the whole world: he was cast out into the earth, and his angels were cast out with him. And I heard a loud voice saying in heaven, Now is come salvation, and strength, and the kingdom of our God, and the power of his Christ: for the accuser of our brethren is cast down, which accused them before our God day and night. And they overcame by the blood of the Lamb, and by the word

72

of their testimony; and they loved not their lives unto the death.

As written in this passage, the "prince of this world" refers to "that old serpent, called the devil, and Satan," who tempted Adam in Eden, who usurped Adam's authority over the world, who eventually deceived the whole world.

Originally, when God created this world, He gave the governing authority to Adam and Eve. In Genesis 1:26 when God created man and woman, He said, "Let us make man in our image, after our likeness: and let them have dominion over the fish of the sea, and over the fowl of the air, and over the cattle, and over all the earth, and over every creeping thing that creepeth upon the earth." Like a king and queen, Adam and Eve were created to rule and govern the world.

Then when was the royal authority usurped and given to the devil? When Adam and Eve disobeyed the commandment of God, listening to the enticing words of the old serpent. As a result of surrendering his will to and obeying the devil, Adam's fellowship with God was broken. He not only became the servant of the devil, but he handed himself and the territory entrusted to him over to the devil.

Since that time "the whole world lieth in wickedness" (1 John 5:19). And from that time on the devil has made a desperate effort to oppose God and interfere with God's plan.

When the devil tempted Jesus in the wilderness, he took Him up to a high mountain and in a moment of time showed Him all the kingdoms of the world. Satan enticed Him saying, "All this power will I give thee, and the glory of them: for that is delivered unto me; and to whomsoever I will I give it. If thou therefore wilt worship me, all shall be thine" (Luke 4:6,7).

Instead of saying that the power of this world was his from the very beginning, the devil confessed that it had been delivered to him. What a tragic day that was!

Since that day when Satan deceived Adam and Eve, the desperate effort of the devil has been to steal and kill and destroy mankind. But God reached out through Jesus Christ to save the world.

The only possible way to save the human race, enslaved as it was to the devil, was for God to prepare a way through which He could legally forgive the original sin and the willful sins that men and women would commit. But because mankind made the choice to rebel against God and submit to the devil, a person's deliverance must be accepted. You and I must choose to receive the good news of God's forgiveness, made possible through Jesus Christ, His only begotten Son.

Thanks to Jesus' sacrificial death, a way is open for man to come back to God and receive the blessing of forgiveness and grace. Hallelujah! If a person turns his or her back on the devil and chooses God, that person will be saved by the overflowing grace of Jesus Christ, be restored as a child of God and recover the authority that was lost long ago.

Because of Jesus' death for us, the deceitful wiles of the devil are revealed before the cross; the devil has gone to ruin and he has been judged. He lost the lawful power to possess man or the world. The devil, who had enslaved the human race and robbed mankind of the world which God had entrusted to them, was judged by the love of God revealed on the cross.

To the devil the cross was a complete defeat—destruction and ruin of his plans with a judgment for final damnation. Through the sacrificial death of Jesus Christ, God has opened the legal way to forgiveness and restoration for all mankind. And the devil is completely incapable of hindering those who are returning to God as they hear the good news of salvation. The devil can only watch in helpless agony.

Then why did Jesus say the Holy Spirit would reprove the world of judgment? There are two meanings in that statement. First, through the sacrifice of Jesus, God forgives the treason of mankind and reproves the devil who enslaved men and women, usurping all the world that God had given to them. Second, it is a touching reproof of God to mankind who, despite the way of salvation that God has prepared, still does not come back to God but continues to forsake the forgiveness freely offered. If anyone persists in this, that person is deprived by the devil of his or her full potential and that person will go to hell.

Whenever people hear the gospel and are saved from the devil's hand, Satan suffers. It ruins his kingdom and he not only desperately tries to hinder people from hearing this gospel, but he also tries to seduce into destruction those who have already believed. But this will never succeed. The forgiveness and love of the cross do not change, and the Holy Spirit continues to spread the word that the devil has been defeated and judged.

Knowing all this, we ought to pray in this way: "O Lord, the Holy Spirit, call me and fill me with Your power. Let me preach this gospel to the uttermost parts of the earth. Let me preach that the prince of this world was already judged two thousand years ago and has no more dominion over mankind."

So now, through the forgiveness that Jesus provided, men and women can leave Satan's territory, stand again before God and recover the royal authority that was delivered to Adam and Eve in the beginning. What a wonderful blessing this is to mankind, and what an appalling judgment this is to the devil.

Speaking of His impending death Jesus said, "Now is the judgment of this world: now shall the prince of this world be cast out" (John 12:31). The devil—who through sin and ignorance gained the opportunity to enter the world and has had ruthless dominion over the world—is even now losing ground moment by moment. Why? Because many are receiving salvation after hearing the gospel.

The cross of Jesus was the complete judgment of the devil, the place where his power was totally broken. How can we help but praise our Lord Jesus who has restored us to be "a chosen generation" and "a royal priesthood" (1 Pet. 2:9)? We cannot help but proclaim with the Holy Spirit that the devil has been judged!

Revealing Salvation's Plan

Unbelievers who have been reproved of sin and righteousness and judgment, and who have been guided into all truth, should now turn from their sinful lives and trust Jesus by faith.

But often their human understanding tells them that the Christian walk is too difficult. They see a gulf that they think cannot be spanned. People who interpret the gospel only with human reason fall into this deep gulf, and they never do pass over to the other side of belief.

How can unbelievers pass over this gulf and enter into the wonderful blessing we believers enjoy as we meditate on the Word and preach it? Remember the words of our Lord Jesus: "With men it is impossible, but not with God" (Mark 10:27).

God easily accomplished this miracle which was impossible for mankind, and He is still working miracles today! The Bible bears witness to the fact that faith cannot be possessed only by human means: "No man can say that Jesus is Lord, but by the Holy Ghost" (1 Cor. 12:3).

How does the Holy Spirit work to allow unbelievers to accept Jesus as their personal Savior? I must admit that it is only through a miracle. New birth is just as much a miracle as was Jesus' conception without a father of flesh and birth through the virgin Mary. "And the angel answered and said unto her, The Holy Ghost shall come upon thee, and the power of the Highest shall overshadow thee: therefore also that holy thing which shall be born of thee shall be called the Son of God" (Luke 1:35).

The incarnation of Jesus is a sheer miracle. The same miracle is necessary for Jesus to come into the spirit of a person. Without the supernatural power of the Holy Spirit, we could never believe in His redeeming work and grace, which defy understanding and reason.

When anyone confesses Jesus as personal Savior, there may or may not be any immediate signs of outward change. But the change occurring in the spiritual realm is indeed enormous. The Holy Spirit of God comes into the spirit of that person and moves within it mysteriously beyond reason and imagination. The Holy Spirit Himself sheds the divine faith (the faith of salvation) in the heart of that person.

Even though that person's brain is full of doubts and uncertainty, the Holy Spirit helps him believe in his heart. The power to believe gushes out, and he easily passes over the previously unpassable gulf that lies between reason and faith. By the power of the Holy Spirit, that person safely enters the bliss of faith. He then studies the Bible, prays and hears sermons—always with the help of the Holy Spirit. The foundation of his faith becomes strong and systematized so that he can enter the bright world of truth, which can then be explained to human reason and intellect.

Again, believing faith is not attained through understanding and knowledge, but through a miracle of the Holy Spirit—when man is pricked in his heart after hearing the Word of God. He then cultivates reasonable understanding and knowledge.

As Paul said, no man can call Jesus Lord but by the Holy

Spirit. Similarly, the preaching of the gospel is impossible without partnership with the Holy Spirit.

Today many churches are losing members and believers are tormented by doubts because man tries to preach the gospel with human effort and calculation. It's impossible! We need the Holy Spirit.

When we try to lead unbelievers to the Lord, we should simply pray earnestly for the miraculous help of the Holy Spirit, becoming His instruments, allowing Him to use us to preach with His fullness.

Not till this is done can unimaginable blessing come before our eyes. We can and will see people flock into the blessed world of faith.

5

Believers and the Holy Spirit

No one can be saved without being empowered with the Word of God and the Holy Spirit. Even after someone is saved he or she cannot have a steady, victorious life of faith and spiritual growth unless he or she keeps on growing in the Word through the ministry of the Holy Spirit.

Many believers are aware vaguely that salvation comes only when one is born again by receiving the gospel as it is shared in the power of the Holy Spirit. But then they try to continue their life of faith with their own human resolution and effort. They suffer from agony—for the good that they want to do, they don't do, but the evil they don't want to do, they do. In the end they utter sighs and cry like Paul: "O wretched man that I am! who shall deliver me from the body of this death?'' (Rom. 7:24).

Our Lord promised again and again that He would send to believers the Comforter, the Holy Spirit, ''that he may abide with you for ever'' (John 14:16). The Spirit would come to ''help our infirmities'' (Rom. 8:26). Just as He promised, seven weeks after He arose from the grave, Jesus sent the Comforter, the Holy Spirit, to this earth.

How does the Holy Spirit take care of the believers who have been born again through the Word and the Spirit?

Bringing Holiness and Helping Our Infirmities

''Likewise the Spirit also helpeth our infirmities: For we know not what we should pray for as we ought: but the Spirit itself maketh intercession for us with groanings which cannot be uttered'' (Rom. 8:26).

Every believer will admit that the problem of sin seriously confronts him with agony after he has believed in the Lord Jesus. In times past when we were unbelievers, ''we all had our conversation [conduct]...in the lusts of our flesh, fulfilling the desires of the flesh and of the mind'' (Eph. 2:3). Then we didn't feel guilty, though we lived in sin. Why? Because the soul was dead before God. But when we receive eternal life, sin becomes a problem to us.

We come to ask such questions as: Can I not help but repeatedly fall into sin even after I am saved? Don't I have the power to overcome sin?

Romans 7 and 8 deal with these questions. Romans 6 teaches the fundamental change that occurs when a person believes in Jesus Christ:

> Know ye not, that so many of us as were baptized into
> Jesus Christ were baptized into his death? Therefore we

are buried with him by baptism into death: that like as Christ was raised up from the dead by the glory of the Father, even so we also should walk in newness of life. For if we have been planted together in the likeness of his death, we shall be also in the likeness of his resurrection: Knowing this, that our old man is crucified with him, that the body of sin might be destroyed, that henceforth we should not serve sin. For he that is dead is freed from sin (Rom. 6:3-7).

What wonderful and blessed news this is! Yet people ask, What shall I do to experience this blessing?

The answer is simple. We all believe and know that we have received remission of sins and salvation by the grace of God.

And what does this grace mean? Grace means that God works for us in person. If we try to save ourselves or help God save us that is not grace. Grace means that we receive by faith what God has accomplished for us on His part.

A person who has accepted Jesus Christ as personal Savior is totally different from one who has accepted only the religious system of Christianity, religious rituals or a moral pattern. Through Christ the old person has been crucified, put to death. The cursed, outcast, corrupt and fallen man who originated from the first Adam has been buried. But through and with Christ, our last Adam, a new person has risen to a new life.

This truth does not end as a theory. As surely as I was born in this world in the same condition as the first son of Adam, so Jesus, the Son of God, was incarnated into this world where He lived for thirty-three years. Just as He was crucified, I too was crucified and buried. I arose a new creature by the power of His resurrection. All who believe in Jesus Christ have experienced this.

The Bible also commands us to change our attitude and

thinking: "Likewise reckon ye also yourselves to be dead indeed unto sin, but alive unto God through Jesus Christ our Lord" (Rom. 6:11). We are to believe that "if any man be in Christ, he is a new creature" (2 Cor. 5:17).

You may wonder why the writer of Romans 7 is still agonizing with the question of sin, when in chapter 6 he died through Christ, was buried and then resurrected a new, righteous man.

The reason is simple. After the old man died and the new man was resurrected, he depended upon the power and merit of Christ. But because he did not really understand his state of regeneration, he fell back into bondage.

Many believers do not realize that just as we had no power to do that which was righteous when we were in sin, so also, after we are born again, we have no power in ourselves to attain to righteousness and holiness. When we start believing that we can be righteous and holy in our own effort, we taste the bitter cup of defeat.

Adam's descendants have held on to his idea—that he could and would do everything for himself. But actually, they have been serving the devil as his slaves, dragged off in defeat. Blind, they do not come out of their delusion and wholly depend upon God. Convinced that they can bring forth salvation and holiness for themselves, they suffer defeat because they simply cannot control their sinful desires.

I can see the believer of Romans 7 fighting a bloody battle against great odds to live a righteous and holy life, trying to keep the law but being deceived by the enticing devil of self. He's so self-centered he uses the word "I" forty times in that chapter. What a proud person! But in the end the Word of God makes us realize an acute truth: No one can possibly overcome sin by himself. The writer finally says, "O wretched man that I am! who shall deliver me from the body of this death?'' (Rom. 7:24).

The answer to this question is simple though it is often under-stood only after hard trials. As salvation comes only by depending upon the merit of the Lord, so the life of righteousness and holiness comes only by relying upon the indwelling power of the Lord of resurrection.

In Romans 8 the apostle clearly states the answer to his own question, ''Who shall deliver me?''

> There is therefore now no condemnation to them which are in Christ Jesus, who walk not after the flesh, but after the Spirit. For the law of the Spirit of life in Christ Jesus hath made me free from the law of sin and death (Rom. 8:1,2).

Paul is saying that the victory belongs to those who are not striving in the range of their own efforts. We who have received new life in Jesus—He who trampled sin, death, the devil and the curse—must be wholly dependent upon Him who is life, righteousness and holiness. When we make Him our personal righteousness and holiness, the ''law of the Spirit of life'' that is revealed and given through Him makes us completely free from the ''law of sin and death.''

When we were born again, our direction in life and purpose for living were converted. The Bible reads, ''In that he died, he died unto sin once: but in that he liveth, he liveth unto God'' (Rom. 6:10).

We should always bear in mind that the life of Christ is not the life for self. Rather, from beginning to end, it is a life lived ''unto God.'' Remember, Adam lived only unto himself. As a result, he became a servant of the devil, the personification of pride.

The reason why born-again Christians still fall into Satan's delusion is that they insist on continuing to live unto themselves instead of unto God.

As long as we are in this deception, living unto ourselves, we can never escape from lust and sin. However, when our first priority is pleasing God in all things and doing His will—when we realize by the Word of God that we are new creatures who are "alive unto God through Jesus Christ" (Rom. 6:11)—the Holy Spirit makes us able to bear the fruit of righteousness and holiness abundantly.

Holiness means being set apart from sin and being in agreement with God. If we depart *from* something, we go *to* something else; if we depart from sin, we should not serve self, but serve God entirely.

While we pass through this process, the selfishness to depend upon one's own efforts and to serve oneself is broken little by little. As a person depends upon the indwelling power of the resurrected Christ and lives only to please and serve God, the Holy Spirit (the Spirit of God's holiness) fills that person with a deeper grace of holiness, making him or her grow more godly.

God comes within us through the Holy Spirit and by working His grace in us, He personally sets us free from the law of sin and death, and enables us to keep the law of God. God not only gave us His law, but He empowers us to keep it through the presence of the Holy Spirit within us. This is grace.

Therefore the apostle Paul said in Galatians 2:20, "I am crucified with Christ: nevertheless I live; yet not I, but Christ liveth in me."

Now it is not I who live. Christ who is in me lives for me, believes for me and acts for me through the Holy Spirit. Knowing this, I just trust that He is changing my heart daily. That's it! This is grace! This is what God works for us and these are the essentials of the gospel!

We can no longer get by with such an excuse as "The spirit indeed is willing, but the flesh is weak" (Matt. 26:41).

We should not only recognize the Holy Spirit and believe Him, but actually welcome Him and allow Him to fill us with Himself so that we automatically keep God's law—not by outward compulsion, but by the power of the Holy Spirit in our inner being. We are not only with the Holy Spirit but the Holy Spirit is clothed with us. Thus the Holy Spirit helps our infirmities and He lives the life of faith through us. What a tremendous truth this is!

Teaching Believers

Just as a child must receive spiritual, moral and intellectual teaching to grow into responsible adulthood, so must a born-again Christian be nourished to grow up in the faith. This newly born believer should grow in the likeness of Christ, and the very person who takes charge of teaching believers is the Holy Spirit: "He shall teach you all things" (John 14:26).

We tend to limit this teaching to knowledge of scholarly doctrine. But the Holy Spirit educates the whole personality of a believer.

Before we came into the world of faith, all of our education was humanistic and learned through the senses. But after a person is born again, the ministry of the Holy Spirit is a revelational education through the Word of God.

The teachings of the Holy Spirit always lead believers toward lessons to be learned. He teaches believers to follow Christ. He enables them to serve the Lord of heaven and earth. He leads them to make pleasing the heavenly Father their highest priority, because only in that is the true worth of life received. And only in pleasing the Father does a person find his true identity as well as everlasting faith, hope and love.

THE HOLY SPIRIT, MY SENIOR PARTNER

The spiritual teaching of the Holy Spirit is in progress naturally, in every field of our human will, feelings and intelligence. Through our will and emotions, the Holy Spirit brings us into the likeness of Christ. Through our intellect He works to make us realize the deeper meanings of the Word of God.

Jesus was at the same time perfect God and perfect man. Therefore in the divine nature of Jesus there existed only perfect beauty—but His human nature needed growth. The Bible acknowledges this by saying, "Jesus increased in wisdom and stature, and in favour with God and man" (Luke 2:52).

And the author of Hebrews said this:

> Who in the days of his flesh, when he had offered up prayers and supplications with strong crying and tears unto him that was able to save him from death, and was heard in that he feared; though he were a Son, yet learned he obedience by the things which he suffered; and being made perfect, he became the author of eternal salvation unto all them that obey him (Heb. 5:7-9).

As this passage shows, even Jesus' human nature learned obedience and was made perfect through diverse trials and sufferings according to the will of God. So also we Christians should be taught by the Holy Spirit, growing and learning from Him about the spiritual life.

The Holy Spirit's teaching of believers can be roughly divided into two methods: through the Word of God and through the experiences of life.

Before Jesus left this world, He repeatedly promised that the Holy Spirit would come to teach the whole truth and enable believers to understand and bear it (see John 16:12-14). Such promises of the Lord were fulfilled in the lives of the disciples after Pentecost.

Before Pentecost, the disciples did not understand the deeper truths of Jesus' teaching. After Jesus was crucified and resurrected, their bewilderment was beyond description; they were at a loss to know what to do. But after they received the Holy Spirit at Pentecost, their lives changed drastically. They not only remembered the teaching of Jesus concerning the Holy Spirit, but they also came to realize the inner meaning of the Word of God. They digested the truths for their own lives so that they might grow.

And so it is with us. Though we try hard to study and comprehend the Word of God, unless we are filled with the Holy Spirit, who in turn gives birth to a longing for His teachings, we can only cling to words that we do not understand. We remain bewildered and lead a fruitless life, lacking the deep gratitude for God's glory that can be obtained through faithful obedience and service to God. We cannot reach our full potential in Christ unless the Holy Spirit of truth leads us to drink the true milk and honey of the Word, which is spirit and life. Human reason cannot understand the Word. Understanding can come only through the revelation of the Holy Spirit.

The Holy Spirit also teaches us through the trials and experiences of everyday life. We learn to desire God's will and follow the example of Christ. The tests and discipline enable us to claim the truth as our own, and allow us to find and realize the deeper understanding of the Word.

We should not belittle or neglect to live out the teachings of the Holy Spirit that we receive through real-life tests and experiences as well as through the Word.

Being born again and filled with the Holy Spirit can be compared to entering the "school" of the Holy Spirit. This school has neither holiday nor vacation. In every situation of life, the Holy Spirit presents Christ as our model in the study of the

Word. The Holy Spirit leads us to imitate and participate in His life. Many times a day, He speaks to us through the Word or through an experience, because school is always in session.

The Bible says that when Jesus came up out of the water after being baptized, the heavens were opened and the Holy Spirit descended upon Him like a dove. Then, after Jesus returned from the Jordan filled with the Holy Spirit, He was led by the Spirit into the wilderness to be tempted by the devil for forty days (see Luke 3:22; 4:1,2).

Of course the Holy Spirit did not lead Jesus to be tempted so as to destroy Him. This temptation of the devil was only to discipline Him.

. Likewise, the Holy Spirit is with us and teaches us—both when we sense the wonderful grace and truth of God and when we feel as if we have been deserted in a wilderness. The Holy Spirit educates us so that our faith—centering on God, depending upon His Word and the love and hope of heaven—may grow.

Under no circumstances should believers who have entered the school of the Holy Spirit be discouraged or move backward. The Bible encourages us by saying, ''Count it all joy when ye fall into divers temptations; knowing this, that the trying of your faith worketh patience. But let patience have her perfect work, that ye may be perfect and entire, wanting nothing'' (James 1:2-4).

Therefore—if we always live a life that pleases God and centers on Him, if we always depend upon the Lord Jesus— the Holy Spirit, who has come to teach us, will make us grow so that we may lack nothing in the knowledge of the Word and of our faith.

Leading Believers

"For as many as are led by the Spirit of God, they are the sons of God" (Rom. 8:14).

The heavenly Father has sent the Holy Spirit to lead born-again believers along the right spiritual paths. The children of God have become people of a spiritual world by regeneration, yet they still live in the physical world in a tabernacle of the flesh. How does one live daily as a child of light in this world of darkness?

It is a difficult problem that cannot be solved by human effort. Yet the Holy Spirit of God easily solves this problem and leads believers into a victorious life. How does this happen?

The big problem believers face today is that of leadership: Is the Holy Spirit their leader or do they lead themselves?

When believers consult me about problems of faith or when they request prayer, I often look closely into their eyes and find that they really aren't looking for help. They have already monopolized the leadership of their lives. They have already made their own plans and decisions, and now they want to ask the Holy Spirit to come and bless their blueprint. These believers are not allowing the Holy Spirit to lead them; they are leading themselves.

If we are to be led by the Holy Spirit, we need to understand the proper relationship between the Holy Spirit and ourselves. The fundamental sin man committed against God is that he disregarded the cosmic order and usurped the place of God. Man served himself, loved himself and lived a life of pride. He not only refused to recognize God in his self-centered world, but he rebelled and left Him.

Even many people who have believed in the Lord Jesus and been born again are still full of pride, that evil root. These people try to take advantage of God and use Him when they need

Him—as one who is there for a single purpose, to bless them.

We can never have a satisfactory communication with the Holy Spirit if we have such a misunderstanding of His purpose in the world and in our lives. If we want to be wonderfully led by God, we must not only believe in Jesus and receive the remission of sins, but we must also allow the Holy Spirit to cut off the roots of pride with a sharp axe of judgment. Then we should bow down before the throne, surrendering ourselves wholly to God without any condition or reservation (soul, mind, flesh, life—present, past and future).

We should allow the Holy Spirit to work out through us what God is pleased with instead of what we are pleased with—for His purpose and not for ours. Unless a drastic change comes, the wonderful guidance which the Holy Spirit can give in every area of our lives can be expected only occasionally.

Believers ought to understand that the Creator ordained order in the universe. Why do we creations try to take advantage of our Maker, trying to be equal with Him by exalting ourselves? This pride is sin. It brings sorrow and the curse.

When we come before the presence of God, we should never try to bring Him down to our level. To God, that pride smells like a piece of putrified meat. Through Christ, God takes hold of me by the power of the Holy Spirit, cleanses and breaks the pride, and then accomplishes His work through me.

That's the secret of being led by the Spirit. The declaration of faith of the apostle Paul—"I live; yet not I, but Christ liveth in me" (Gal. 2:20)—is the foundation of life for sincere and true believers. When we wait upon God, waiting for and serving Him as servants bowing before the Master's feet, God does not endeavor to lead us with humility. He takes possession of us and lives through us. Only in such a life can we have true rest, joy, and a firm belief and hope in life. When we know that God through the Holy Spirit rules and leads in every area of our lives, we can sing joyfully even when our days seem like dark nights.

The Holy Spirit who has come to us works to change our lives in this way. As we surrender to Him, we naturally become the splendid sons of God who are "led by the Spirit of God," as described in Romans 8:14. Moreover, every son and daughter have the qualification and capacity to be led by the Spirit of God. Praise His name!

Comforting Believers

Have you ever felt torn apart by the cares of life? You thought you were about to go under, but then you heard kind words of comfort from dear parents, family or close friends? Comfort is like oil poured on wounds and it gives new courage.

Yet there is a limit to human comfort. There is a "bottomless pit" of despair where human comfort cannot reach; there are times when only God can reach us.

Before Jesus left this world, He promised the sorrowing, uneasy, despondent disciples, "I will not leave you comfortless; I will come to you" (John 14:18). While Jesus was with His disciples, He was not only their unfailing Lord; He was a Comforter who took care of them. He provided food for them, healed them and kept them free from the attacks of the enemy. But when Jesus left them, the disciples felt like comfortless orphans. They didn't understand Jesus' promise: "I will pray the Father, and he shall give you another Comforter, that he may abide with you for ever" (John 14:16). Here the Holy Spirit is called the Comforter.

On the day of Pentecost, the disciples were all filled with the Holy Spirit and began to speak with other tongues, as the Spirit gave them utterance. After they had experienced this wonderful incident, their hearts became full of comfort, peace and boldness. The Holy Spirit, the Comforter, was within them.

From that day on, their hearts knew neither loneliness nor sorrow, neither oppressed emotions nor despair, though they were slandered, beaten and put into prison. The Holy Spirit was there, supplying them with the unending comfort of God. They could praise God even in tribulation and affliction.

How could Stephen, the first martyr, possess enough faith to bless his murderers instead of cursing them? Because his heart was full of comfort. How could Paul and Silas in a Philippi prison—beaten, hungry and bound fast by fetters—begin to sing midnight praises unto God? Because their hearts were overflowing with the comfort of the Holy Spirit.

Do you remember the rest of that story? God responded to the praises and prayers of Paul and Silas, and caused an earthquake to shake the foundation of the prison, swinging open all the doors. Their bands were loosed and they received freedom. By morning, the family of the prison keeper was saved. The Holy Spirit came and gave profound comfort to the torn, hurt and bleeding souls.

The apostle Paul wrote to the Corinthians concerning God's comfort through the power of the Holy Spirit:

> Blessed be God, even the Father of our Lord Jesus Christ, the Father of mercies, and the God of all comfort; who comforteth us in all our tribulation, that we may be able to comfort them which are in any trouble, by the comfort wherewith we ourselves are comforted of God. For as the sufferings of Christ abound in us, so our consolation also aboundeth by Christ (2 Cor. 1:3-5).

The comfort coming from God through the Holy Spirit allows

us to overcome tribulations and ordeals.

In the first church I pioneered there was an elderly woman who had been widowed when still young. Through much sacrifice and suffering she had brought up a daughter. When this daughter married and started her own family, her mother went to live with her to take care of the house. After childbirth the daughter's heart was weak. That mother prayed earnestly to God for her daughter's healing. The widow experienced the fullness of the Holy Spirit, but the daughter died.

It seemed the mother's world had collapsed. For her daughter she had sacrificed her own desires of life, and now that daughter was gone. What words could comfort this woman in the depths of her despair?

When her daughter's lifeless body was laid out in the house, as is our custom in Korea, I was called to lead the funeral service there. When I walked into that house I knew something had changed. Previously, the woman had been inconsolable. But now the face of that old woman was radiant instead of full of despair. She even comforted me, the servant of the Lord, saying that we didn't have to worry about her daughter for she had already gone to her eternal home in heaven. She assured me that the young woman was in the bosom of God. She sang praises with strength and even danced with joy. Who could have given this wonderful comfort to her?

Only the Holy Spirit of God can and does wonderfully heal painful wounds by pouring oil on them. He gives the power to stand up and march onward, singing a triumphant song.

When we are filled with the Holy Spirit and learn to walk with Him, deep comfort, which the world does not know or understand, overflows in our souls. We can receive new strength to conquer any circumstances. We become believers that can offer solace to all afflicted people.

THE HOLY SPIRIT, MY SENIOR PARTNER

Confirming That We Are God's Children

"And because ye are sons, God hath sent forth the Spirit of his Son unto your hearts, crying, Abba, Father" (Gal. 4:6).

To be a father means to be the author of a child's life and the cause of that child's being. Only one man can be my father in that sense of the word.

But God also is my Father in the faith—the author and cause of my resurrected, or born-again, being. Our Christian faith is not a religion as a lot of people misunderstand it. Can you call the birth of a baby a religion?

The Christian faith is not a religion but an experience with the Lord Jesus Christ. I experienced the new birth. I was born of God. God became my Father and I became His own son. All the steps of growth we take in the church (the lessons preceding baptism, baptism itself, church membership, the rites) may be external helps to become better children of God, but they are not the same as being born into God's family by the power of the Holy Spirit.

We read in the Gospel of John: "But as many as received him, to them gave he power to become the sons of God, even to them that believe on his name: which were born, not of blood, nor of the will of the flesh, nor of the will of man, but of God" (1:12,13). As this word clearly shows, we cannot become children of God by our blood or the will of flesh or the will of man, however hard we may try. You are born as a child of God only when you are born again by the power of the Holy Spirit. Without the experience of a cleansed heart you cannot obtain the authority to become a child of God.

James 1:18 says, "Of his own will begat he us with the word of truth, that we should be a kind of firstfruits of his creatures." You are born of God when you receive the word of God by the power of the Holy Spirit.

Even Jesus Himself said to Nicodemus, "Verily, verily, I say unto thee, Except a man be born again, he cannot see the kingdom of God." When Nicodemus asked, "How can a man be born when he is old? Can he enter the second time into his mother's womb, and be born?" Jesus answered, "Verily, verily, I say unto thee, Except a man be born of water and of the Spirit, he cannot enter into the kingdom of God. That which is born of the flesh is flesh; and that which is born of the Spirit is spirit" (see John 3:3-6).

We are born of God as spiritual children through the Word of God by the power of the Holy Spirit just as we are born of our parents of flesh, receiving physical life.

When we are born again the Holy Spirit reveals to us our intimate relationship to God, our Father.

A woman with whom I am well-acquainted once told me the following story: Because her sister had no children, this woman sent her own daughter to her sister's home for adoption. But the daughter would not call her aunt "Mother." No matter how hard they tried to persuade her to say the word, she would not call her aunt "Mother." She always made an inarticulate utterance when she addressed her foster mother. Refusing to call her aunt "Mother," she could not become her adopted daughter.

That same parent-child bond works in the spiritual world. Through the Word and the Holy Spirit, we come to call God "Abba, Father" out of a tingling instinct in our hearts.

The Bible shows clearly that the Holy Spirit of God is doing this work. In Romans 8 we read: "Ye have not received the spirit of bondage again to fear; but ye have received the Spirit of adoption, whereby we cry, Abba, Father. The Spirit itself beareth witness with our spirit, that we are the children of God" (vv. 15,16). In our hearts by the revelation of the Holy Spirit

95

we know that God has become our Father and we have become His children.

This assurance doesn't come by the rites of any church but by the Holy Spirit Himself, who comes upon our hearts and reveals it to us. Without the work of the Holy Spirit, we could become only religious people, not God's very own children. We could be believers, but not members of the family of God.

Many churches today are cool and have no fervent love toward God because the members come to church merely as religious persons—having no firm belief in their hearts by the revelation of the Spirit that God has become their Father.

Truth dawns in our hearts neither by might nor by power but by the revelation of the Holy Spirit when we are born again by the Spirit of God.

6

The Baptism of the Holy Spirit

Regeneration Always Comes First

Regeneration is what Jesus referred to when He told Nicodemus, "Ye must be born again" (John 3:7).

Nicodemus was a ruler of the Pharisees, a group of Jews who kept the strict law and religious rites. Not finding truth and satisfaction in his religion, he came to Jesus at night. In response to a statement by Nicodemus, Jesus made a disturbing declaration: "Except a man be born again, he cannot see the kingdom of God" (John 3:3).

Nicodemus had tried to be admitted to the kingdom of God by keeping the law and religious rites, by cultivating virtue through self-improvement and effort. All his hard work seemed to crumble in a moment.

So Nicodemus asked hastily, "How can a man be born when he is old? Can he enter the second time into his mother's womb, and be born?" (John 3:4).

Jesus answered that question by explaining clearly the law of rebirth:

> Verily, verily, I say unto thee, Except a man be born of water and of the Spirit, he cannot enter into the kingdom of God. That which is born of the flesh is flesh; and that which is born of the Spirit is spirit. Marvel not that I said unto thee, Ye must be born again (vv. 5-7).

Here Jesus taught that salvation could not be achieved by a person's own effort, self-improvement or religious celebration. Rather it takes place when God brings about rebirth at the center of a person's being.

Something new must happen. Think of it this way: However well a monkey imitates man, it cannot become a human being because monkeys are fundamentally different from humans in the level of their existence.

John 1:13 declares that to become children of God we must be born of God: "Which were born, not of blood, nor of the will of the flesh, nor of the will of man, but of God."

Therefore salvation means that a man of flesh is born again through the Holy Spirit by the grace of God and essentially becomes a spiritual being. It is what God does for man. Salvation is possible only by the gift of God.

By that gift we become "partakers of the divine nature" (2 Pet. 1:4) through the grace of God and have the eternal life of God.

What then does it mean that God enables sinners to be born again by water and the Holy Spirit?

Some people insist that "born of water" here means the

physical baptism of water. But the Bible attaches greater importance to the meaning of this phrase. Of course I do not say that water baptism is a light or unnecessary act. Can it be true that God commands an unnecessary thing?

The meaning of *water* here is, above all, "washing." The Bible elsewhere teaches that we are washed by the Word of God. Jesus said to His disciples, "Now ye are clean through the word which I have spoken unto you" (John 15:3); and Paul wrote, "That he might sanctify and cleanse it [the church] with the washing of water by the word" (Eph. 5:26).

When Jesus says we must be "born of water and of the Spirit," He is referring to the Word of God and the Holy Spirit. Who could be the Word of God but Jesus Himself (see John 1:1,2,14)?

Further on in His conversation with doubting Nicodemus, Jesus referred to Himself: "As Moses lifted up the serpent in the wilderness, even so must the Son of man be lifted up: That whosoever believeth in him should not perish, but have eternal life" (John 3:14).

Only the precious blood of Jesus, who is the living Word, can make us clean—and that blood is the very word which cleanses us.

But Jesus said we are born again "of water"—or the Word—"and the Spirit." Then what does the Holy Spirit do?

Ezekiel 36:26 describes beautifully how sinners are changed into new creatures by the Spirit of God: "A new heart also will I give you, and a new spirit will I put within you: and I will take away the stony heart out of your flesh, and I will give you an heart of flesh" (see also Ezek. 11:19).

Today our Savior Jesus Christ can neither be understood nor explained except through the Holy Spirit, the author of miracles of salvation.

He is the administrative agent of God's salvation, reproving us of our sin through the Word and revealing Christ, who becomes our righteousness and declares the judgment to Satan (see John 16:8).

In John 16:14, Jesus showed that He revealed Himself only through the vessel of the Holy Spirit: "He shall glorify me: for he shall receive of mine, and shall shew it unto you."

The Holy Spirit carries out the new creative work that transforms a person by leading him to receive eternal life and the nature of God. But the Holy Spirit goes a step beyond regeneration, and that's what the baptism of the Holy Spirit is all about.

Regeneration is not the same experience as the baptism of (or with) the Holy Spirit. Of course, both regeneration and the baptism of the Holy Spirit can happen at the same time. But in other cases there is an interval of time between the two experiences. Let's take a biblical look at the difference between regeneration and the baptism of the Holy Spirit.

In the Bible there is clear mention of born-again believers who had not received the baptism with the Holy Spirit.

Before Jesus' death His disciples had already received eternal life, for Jesus called them in person and they obeyed Him, believing that He was the Son of God.

Jesus said, "Verily, verily, I say unto you, He that heareth my word, and believeth on him that sent me, hath everlasting life" (John 5:24). Jesus also testified in John 13:10 that His disciples were all clean except Judas Iscariot. And when the seventy disciples returned from preaching and told Jesus how the devils were subject to them, Jesus admitted that the seventy disciples had already received everlasting life (see Luke 10:20).

But Jesus did not say that they had received the baptism of the Holy Spirit from the moment they believed (as some theologians today claim). It's quite clear that they hadn't yet received the fullness of the Spirit. Before He ascended into heaven, Jesus told His disciples that they should not depart from Jerusalem yet: "Wait for the promise of the Father, which ye have heard of me. For John truly baptized with water; but ye shall be baptized with the Holy Ghost not many days hence" (Acts 1:4,5).

Some people agree that the believing disciples needed the baptism of the Holy Spirit, but they say that was only because they were believers before Pentecost. The argument goes that any believer since that Pentecost when the church was born and the Holy Spirit descended receives the baptism of the Holy Spirit at the time of conversion.

But New Testament accounts show such a theory to be wrong.

Acts 8:5-13 describes the scene of deacon Philip preaching the gospel in Samaria. The people there "with one accord gave heed unto those things which Philip spake, hearing and seeing the miracles which he did." As a result, "unclean spirits, crying with loud voice, came out of many that were possessed with them: and many taken with palsies, and that were lame, were healed. And there was great joy in that city." The account goes on to say that a great number of men and women believed the gospel and were baptized.

But the next passage says that though they believed and were baptized, they were by no means baptized with the Holy Spirit:

> Now when the apostles which were at Jerusalem heard that Samaria had received the word of God, they sent unto them Peter and John: Who, when they were come down, prayed for them, that they might receive the Holy Ghost: (For as yet he was fallen upon none of them: only they were baptized in the name of the Lord Jesus.) Then laid they their hands on them, and they received the Holy Ghost (Acts 8:14-17).

This indicates that to believe and be born again is distinctly different from receiving the Holy Spirit.

Acts 9:5-17 tells a vivid account of Paul's conversion and experience of being filled with the Holy Spirit, which didn't happen simultaneously.

With a letter of authority from the high priests, Saul and his friends went toward Damascus, the capital of Syria, to persecute those who believed in Jesus and bring them into prison.

But when he and his followers came near Damascus, "suddenly there shined round about him a light from heaven" which blinded him. Having heard the voice of the Lord Jesus, Saul fell to the earth and confessed that Jesus was the Lord. He went into Damascus a different man, obeying God.

Saul fasted and prayed for three days. From this we see that he had become a new creature in Christ. Then Ananias put his hands on Saul and prayed that he be filled with the Holy Spirit, which he was.

Another example is the church at Ephesus which had been established through the eloquent preaching of Apollos. But when Paul visited that church, he found it struggling and weak. The first question Paul asked was this: "Have ye received the Holy Ghost since ye believed?" (Acts 19:2). Paul knew that if they had received the Holy Spirit, they wouldn't have been so powerless and feeble with only twelve or so members.

If Christians always received the Holy Spirit when they believed, why would Paul have deliberately asked the unnecessary question, "Have ye received the Holy Ghost since ye believed?" Faith does not mean that one automatically receives the fullness of the Holy Spirit. It is something a believer should pray and ask for.

In fact, first-century Spirit-filled believers thought that Christians who weren't Spirit-filled lacked a necessary qualification for service. Because of this, new believers as a rule prayed earnestly to receive the Holy Spirit.

Before the believers at Ephesus received the Holy Spirit, the church was miserably weak and sick. But after the people received the fullness of the Holy Spirit through Paul's ministry, a wonderful vitality and power of faith exploded in their midst. After a while it became a famous church that filled all of Asia Minor with the Word of God.

When we take all these accounts into consideration, we can see that regeneration and the baptism with the Holy Spirit are two distinctly different experiences.

Regeneration is the experience of receiving the life of the Lord by being grafted into the body of Christ through the Holy Spirit and the Scriptures. The baptism of the Holy Spirit is the experience in which Jesus fills believers with the power of God for ministry, service and victorious living.

Regeneration grants a person everlasting life, while the baptism of the Holy Spirit grants regenerate believers the power of God to preach Christ.

Christians today are not powerless, sick and spiritless because they are not born again, but because they have not received the fullness of the Holy Spirit, the tremendous power of God for service.

Without the baptism of the Holy Spirit the church today can never display God's power as did the early church—a combative, challenging and victorious power to evangelize a generation. For this reason, we should renounce the foolish, weak and lethargic excuse that all believers immediately receive the Holy Spirit when they believe. Rather we should pray to receive the fullness of the Holy Spirit.

THE HOLY SPIRIT, MY SENIOR PARTNER

What Did God Promise?

If a Christian is to have power and authority to carry out the ministry and service of God, he or she must have the baptism of the Holy Spirit.

In Old Testament times God gave the wonderful anointing of the Holy Spirit (which corresponds to today's baptism of the Holy Spirit) to His specially chosen vessels: kings, priests, judges, prophets and deliverers of the Israelites, whom He used according to His ordained will. But at that time only a few people were anointed with the power of God, so ordinary people could not even dream of such grace.

Yet God prophesied that in the future the call for salvation would come to all people; He would also give the anointing of the Holy Spirit to anyone who answered the call of God.

The most vivid and prominent of many prophecies is written in Joel 2:

> And it shall come to pass afterward, that I will pour out my spirit upon all flesh: and your sons and your daughters shall prophesy, your old men shall dream dreams, your young men shall see visions: And also upon the servants and upon the handmaids in those days will I pour out my spirit (vv. 28,29).

The excellent and wonderful point of this prophecy is that God declared through the prophet Joel that in the future He would provide salvation not only for Israel but for everyone regardless of nation, race or status; He would give the fullness of the Holy Spirit to all peoples.

Joel was a prophet of Judah who lived some 770 years before Christ. Jews of those days were extremely exclusive: God's chosen people were the Israelites. Jehovah God was not the God of the Gentiles; furthermore He could not become the Savior of Gentiles.

In such a climate, this prophecy told that in the future God would give His Spirit not only to Jewish people but to all flesh. There would be no regard for sex and age. God even promised that He would give His Spirit to humble servants and hand-maids, to prisoners taken from foreign countries, to slaves bought with money—people who were ill-treated and despised, in the lowest position of Jewish society.

Yet about eight hundred years later this prophecy was fulfilled literally.

Forty days after Jesus rose from the dead, He commanded His disciples to stay in Jerusalem: "Wait for the promise of the Father, which ye have heard of me. For John truly baptized with water, but ye shall be baptized with the Holy Ghost not many days hence" (Acts 1:4,5).

These words make it clear that the prophecy of Joel and the cry of John the Baptist at the Jordan—"I indeed baptize you with water; but one mightier than I cometh, the latchet of whose shoes I am not worthy to unloose: he shall baptize you with the Holy Ghost and with fire" (Luke 3:16)—refer to the life and work of Jesus.

The disciples of Jesus, following the commandment of the Lord, gathered together in the upper room in Jerusalem and continued to pray.

The Jewish calendar tells us how long they prayed. Jesus died at the Passover feast. The Holy Spirit came upon the disciples on the day of Pentecost, a feast celebrated fifty days after Passover. Jesus had shown Himself to His disciples for forty days between His resurrection and ascension. So the disciples gathered together in Jerusalem for prayer for about ten days.

The Bible thus describes the wonderful miracle that came upon the disciples at Pentecost:

> And when the day of Pentecost was fully come, they were all with one accord in one place. And suddenly there came a sound from heaven as of a rushing mighty wind, and it filled all the house where they were sitting. And there appeared unto them cloven tongues like as of fire, and it sat upon each of them. And they were all filled with the Holy Ghost, and began to speak with other tongues, as the Spirit gave them utterance (Acts 2:1-4).

Peter, immediately after he had received the baptism of the Holy Spirit, stood before a great multitude of people flocked around him and lifted up his voice. He claimed that this was that which had been spoken of by the prophet Joel eight hundred years before—that God would pour out His Spirit upon all flesh.

In Peter's quotation of the prophecy of Joel, the Holy Spirit clarified the time frame (Joel's "afterward") by saying "in the last days," indicating the last days started when Jesus ascended into heaven; the time had come when God would pour His Spirit out upon all flesh.

Peter gave bigger and more wonderful promises to those who heard him preach and then repented:

> Repent, and be baptized every one of you in the name of Jesus Christ for the remission of sins, and ye shall receive the gift of the Holy Ghost. For the promise is unto you, and to your children, and to all that are afar off, even as many as the Lord our God shall call (Acts 2:38,39).

Let's examine this passage by dividing it into several parts.

First, this word contains a national promise to Jews: "every one of you" refers to the Jews who were hearing Peter preach.

Second, Peter gives a promise to future generations of Jewish people: "unto you, and to your children."

Third, the promise relates to the whole world: "to all that are afar off." Jewish rabbis of those days used that expression when they spoke of heathens—or foreigners.

Fourth, the promise refers to all times: "as many as" applies not only to everyone regardless of nation, race, sex, age, possessions or rank—but also to everyone until the end of time, when Christ comes back to earth. What a wonderful promise: God will pour out the Holy Spirit not only in the days of the apostles but throughout the whole age of grace, even now.

Phenomena That Accompany the Spirit

By examining the biblical record of the personal experiences of those who were baptized with the Holy Spirit, we can uncover sound knowledge concerning the phenomena that appear when the Holy Spirit is received.

When Christians want to receive the baptism of the Holy Spirit, many ask a sincere question: What evidence will appear and give them the assurance that they have been baptized with the Holy Spirit?

I know I tried every means and left no stone unturned, earnestly praying to receive the Holy Spirit. During this time I would sometimes enjoy wonderful peace and joy of heart. I could sometimes boldly preach the gospel in the marketplaces, in busses or in streetcars. I often had that experience of feeling that the Word of God was as sweet as honey. In spite of all this, I did not have the assurance in my heart that I had received the fullness of the Holy Spirit, and I did not know why.

Full of questions, I visited many respected servants of the Lord, but I failed to receive a satisfying answer. Finally, I decided to find the answer in the Word of God. But where in the

Bible could the teachings concerning the baptism of the Holy Spirit be found?

Material seemed limited. In the Old Testament and in the Gospels "the Holy Ghost was not yet given; because that Jesus was not yet glorified" (John 7:39). In the epistles the teaching is mainly for believers who had already received the fullness of the Spirit; they contain no direct scenes of the baptism of the Holy Spirit.

Such scenes are recorded only in Acts, and so I decided to study that book with an unprejudiced, honest and open heart.

As a result of that study, the truth of the Word of God was as clear to me as the bright sunlight, and the fullness of the Holy Spirit I had experienced was accompanied by indisputable evidence. The deep feelings I initially felt at the time I received the fullness of the Holy Spirit became deeper as time went by.

Let's examine the accounts of the saints in Acts who received the baptism of the Holy Spirit.

Pentecost

The most wonderful incident was the baptism of the Holy Spirit of the 120 disciples on the day of Pentecost.

When they received the fullness of the Holy Spirit, they must have known beyond question that they had received the gift Jesus had told them to wait for. Otherwise, why would they have stopped waiting and gone out into the front lines of gospel preaching? According to the Bible, 120 disciples without exception stopped waiting for the wonderful experience and had the conviction that they had received the Holy Spirit. How could everyone have had that experience simultaneously? Because the fullness of the Holy Spirit had included not only an outward experience but also an inner assurance.

Let's consider the phenomena that appeared in the upper room when the Holy Spirit came down on Pentecost (Acts 2:2-4).

1. "Suddenly there came a sound from heaven as of a rushing mighty wind."

2. "There appeared unto them cloven tongues like as of fire, and it sat upon each of them."

3. "And they were all filled with the Holy Ghost, and began to speak with other tongues, as the Spirit gave them utterance."

From the above progression we can see that before the disciples experienced the baptism of the Holy Spirit, they heard a sound of wind and saw cloven tongues like as of fire. Then the sign of speaking with other tongues followed the experience of receiving the fullness of the Holy Spirit.

With these signs, the 120 disciples' experience of receiving the baptism of the Holy Spirit was certain beyond question. Knowing what had happened, their representative, Peter, spoke before the crowd of people gathered together. Speaking of Jesus, Peter said, "Therefore being by the right hand of God exalted, and having received of the Father the promise of the Holy Ghost, he hath shed forth this, which ye now see and hear" (Acts 2:33).

Peter was saying that there was objective proof of the experience of the baptism of the Holy Spirit.

We also should bear witness to our experience of the fullness of the Holy Spirit, not in general terms, but like Peter with that which one can see and hear. If we don't have evident proof—if we continue the spiritual struggle, not being sure whether we have received the Holy Spirit or not—how can we become bold and powerful witnesses?

Samaria

The book of Acts mentions a second experience of the fullness of the Holy Spirit—in Samaria.

After deacon Stephen was martyred in Jerusalem, great persecution against the church continued. Most of the church, except the apostles, was scattered abroad throughout the regions of Judea and Samaria.

Philip went down to the city of Samaria and preached Christ. As a result many believed in Christ and were baptized in water. Many possessed by unclean spirits were delivered; many lame and many afflicted with palsies were healed (see Acts 8:5-8).

Despite these miracles, it seems that Philip did not have the gift of helping people receive the baptism of the Holy Spirit. The Bible goes on to say:

> When the apostles which were at Jerusalem heard that Samaria had received the word of God, they sent unto them Peter and John: who, when they were come down, prayed for them, that they might receive the Holy Ghost: (For as yet he was fallen upon none of them: only they were baptized in the name of the Lord Jesus.) then laid they their hands on them, and they received the Holy Ghost (Acts 8:14-17).

Some readers will ask, "But were there external signs when believers in Samaria received the Holy Spirit?"

When we look more deeply into the Word, we see that some unusual things happened that day.

A sorcerer named Simon attended Philip's big salvation and healing crusade, and was greatly moved as he saw the power of God revealed. He accepted Jesus as his Savior and was even baptized.

Then Peter and John came down from Jerusalem, laying their hands on the believers, who then received the Holy Ghost. Now Simon was so amazed by this that he offered them money, saying "Give me also this power, that on whomsoever I lay hands, he may receive the Holy Ghost" (v. 19).

He was severely rebuked by the apostle Peter when he tried

to buy the gift of God with money. But in his behavior there is a tacit lesson which cannot be disregarded. This sorcerer Simon saw all of these things happening: People repenting and confessing their sins were changed and filled with joy. Unclean spirits crying with loud voices came out of many. Many who had been afflicted with palsies or who were lame were totally healed. At the sight of these miracles Simon didn't try to buy such power with money. It was when Peter and John came down and laid hands on believers to receive the Holy Spirit that Simon tried to buy the power.

Why? The answer is very simple: Because a special sign appeared to the Samaritans who received the Holy Spirit through the laying on of hands by Peter and John. Had the Spirit passed calmly and quietly, Simon wouldn't have hurried to offer money.

What did the sorcerer see as a result of the prayer of Peter and John? He must have seen and heard those believers speak with other tongues and praise God.

We cannot help but infer this, because in Philip's crusade all the signs had occurred except one—that of speaking with other tongues.

Don't misunderstand me. Speaking with tongues and the baptism of the Holy Spirit are not synonymous. Some people today mistakenly say that the Assemblies of God teach this. Let me put it this way: In the time of the apostles, whenever God poured out the Holy Spirit upon exemplary churches, He always provided external signs which both those who received the Holy Spirit and objective spectators could spontaneously feel, see and hear. Almost without exception, as the final and most common sign, the recipients spoke with other tongues.

It is clear that the Pentecostal experience of Samaria, which occurred about eight years after the apostles were baptized with the Holy Spirit in Jerusalem, was an experience accompanied by wonderful signs.

Cornelius

The third recorded experience of receiving the fullness of the Holy Spirit took place in the house of Cornelius. After leaving Samaria Peter went down to Joppa and tarried there with Simon, a tanner. One day at the sixth hour Peter went up to the housetop to pray:

> He became very hungry, and would have eaten: but while they made ready, he fell into a trance, and saw heaven opened, and a certain vessel descending unto him, as it had been a great sheet knit at the four corners, and let down to the earth: wherein were all manner of fourfooted beasts of the earth, and wild beasts, and creeping things, and fowls of the air. And there came a voice to him, Rise, Peter; kill, and eat. But Peter said, Not so, Lord; for I have never eaten any thing that is common or unclean. And the voice spake unto him again the second time, What God hath cleansed, that call not thou common (Acts 10:10-15).

This happened three times before the vessel was drawn up into heaven. As Peter contemplated what this vision might mean, messengers sent from Cornelius knocked on the door.

It seems God had sent an angel to the Gentile Cornelius in a vision, preparing Cornelius to hear the word of salvation and grace. According to the direction of the angel, Cornelius sent messengers to Peter in Joppa. When Peter heard the story his own vision made sense to him.

Peter, an obstinate Jew, had always thought it unlawful to keep company with or visit in the home of someone of another nation. If God had not clearly commanded him to go, Peter by no means would have gone to the house of Cornelius.

But God had said clearly that since He would henceforth make Gentiles clean through faith in Christ, Peter should not call common what God had cleansed. That's how the close-minded Jewish thinking of Peter was changed.

Thus God opened a way, the Pentecostal way, for Gentiles, the people gathered together at the house of the heathen centurion Cornelius, to receive salvation and the fullness of the Holy Spirit through faith in Christ.

Let us look carefully into this encounter, when the Holy Spirit came down upon those Gentiles in the home of Cornelius. Peter preached to the people gathered in the house. He started with the prophecy of John the Baptist, then covered the ministry of Jesus, including His death and resurrection. Peter concluded, "To him gave all the prophets witness, that through his name whosoever believeth in him shall receive remission of sins" (Acts 10:43).

Just as Peter spoke these words, the Holy Spirit suddenly came down upon all the people who heard it.

> While Peter yet spake these words, the Holy Ghost fell on all them which heard the word. And they of the circumcision which believed were astonished, as many as came with Peter, because that on the Gentiles also was poured out the gift of the Holy Ghost. For they heard them speak with tongues, and magnify God (Acts 10:44-46).

As soon as the people there heard the word of truth, that salvation is obtained by believing in Jesus Christ, they believed and uttered amen to the amazing power of the Holy Spirit.

How could other people know and testify that the Gentiles in the house of Cornelius had received the Holy Spirit? When we read the biblical account impartially without any prejudice, the proof is evident. Despite the fact that the stubborn Jews tried to believe that salvation and the fullness of the Holy Spirit were not for the Gentiles, the work of God so wonderfully developed that they could not deny it, "for they heard them speak with tongues, and magnify God" (Acts 10:46).

Note again Acts 10:45 and 46. In this passage the Greek word *for* is a casual conjunction, signifying "seeing that" or "since." The circumcised Jewish Christians were astonished, "for [or *because* or *since*] they heard them speak with tongues, and magnify God."

This indicates that early Christians saw tongues as an external, objective sign of the fullness of the Holy Spirit.

Ephesus

The fourth incident in Acts concerning the fullness of the Holy Spirit took place in Ephesus. About forty years had passed since the first outpouring of the Holy Spirit in the upper room in Jerusalem on the day of Pentecost.

The Spirit-filled disciples now preached the gospel with strength, clothed with great power from heaven.

As a result, they endured many persecutions and tribulations, but the persecutions and tribulations could not stop them.

The gospel had shaken Judea; it had swept over Samaria; now it was advancing to the uttermost parts of the earth, largely due to the efforts of the apostle Paul.

Before he became a Christian and an apostle, Paul—then known as Saul—had persecuted the church with a fierce passion. He had bound believers and cast them into prison and even killed some. But he could not forget one scene—the stoning of deacon Stephen. As rocks and abusive language and slander were hurled at Stephen, he showed no expression of resistance or retaliation. Instead, Stephen's face shone as that of an angel. As Stephen died, he was even praying that God would forgive and bless those who stoned him. It was a scene Saul could not then understand.

But Saul's persecution of the church and his oppression of the believers became even more fierce. With special authority from the high priest in Jerusalem, he was on his way to wreak havoc on the church in Damascus when another experience shook him.

The Scripture tells the story in detail. As Saul traveled to Damascus, he was overcome by a light from heaven. Now it is said that the brilliant noon sun in Damascus is like a rain shower. But the light that shone upon Saul was still more brilliant than that, causing him to go blind and fall to the ground. As he fell to the ground he heard the voice of Jesus: "Saul, Saul, why persecutest thou me?" (Acts 9:4). Still blind, Saul had to be led into Damascus. For three days he fasted and prayed for repentance. Later a believer by the name of Ananias prayed for Saul's sight to be restored.

Saul's name was soon changed to Paul, and forty years after Pentecost he went to Ephesus to preach. When he met certain believers in that city, they remembered his persecution of the church and many were fearful of him.

From the standpoint of spiritual life these few believers were lifeless, reduced to a skeleton of rituals and formalism. Figuratively speaking, it was as if they were breathing their last.

What was the first question the great apostle Paul asked these people?

It is a question to which today's churches—bound by ceremonies, formalism and human-centered ways of thinking—should incline their ears: "Have ye received the Holy Ghost since ye believed?" (Acts 19:2).

Many people who want to hide their powerlessness by justifying their theology are well-prepared to answer this question.

With ease they quickly say, "Of course, we received the Holy Spirit when we believed." But a little closer look in the Bible reveals the foolishness of this answer. If we automatically received the Holy Spirit when we first believed why would the apostle Paul have gone to all the trouble of asking the question?

Salvation is received through regeneration by believing in the work of the Holy Spirit, but authority and power can only be received when a born-again Christian receives the fullness of the Holy Spirit after believing. The disciples in Ephesus must have been honest believers. When they were asked by the apostle Paul, they held nothing back from him: "We have not so much as heard whether there be any Holy Ghost" (Acts 19:2).

What a miserable state they were in not to have so much as heard whether there be any Holy Ghost!

As soon as the apostle Paul heard that, he clearly preached the gospel of salvation of Jesus Christ and gave them water baptism in the name of Jesus.

Would Paul have given water baptism to those who were not born again? No. Christians in Ephesus were certainly believers who had accepted Christ Jesus as Savior, but Paul did not regard them as having received the baptism of the Holy Spirit.

Paul then had a prayer meeting for one reason: to ask for the baptism of the Holy Spirit for these people. Does our church today have such a special prayer meeting to receive the baptism of the Holy Spirit?

When Paul laid his hands on them, the Holy Spirit came upon them. The Bible describes that scene in this way: "When Paul had laid his hands upon them, the Holy Ghost came on them; and they spake with tongues, and prophesied" (Acts 19:6).

Summary

Isn't it significant that the gifts of speaking in tongues and prophecy followed right after the coming of the Holy Spirit? The Scripture can neither be broken nor should it be wrestled with. When we study scenes in which the Holy Spirit came down in the early church, filling the lives of believers, we can find one indisputable common sign. What is that?

We saw that wind, fire and tongues were present in John Mark's upper room on the day of Pentecost. It is inferred that these same signs were evident in Samaria also. At the house of Cornelius, believers spoke in tongues as they praised God. Later, people spoke with tongues and prophesied in Ephesus. Probably everyone who observed these biblical incidents in which the fullness of the Holy Spirit was received would say that the believers spoke in other tongues as the Holy Spirit gave utterance.

Of course, I repeat that speaking in tongues in itself is not the fullness of the Holy Spirit, but as confirmed in the Scriptures tongues is the common external sign that a person has received the fullness of the Holy Spirit.

7

Receiving the Baptism of the Holy Spirit

If we are to look into how one receives the baptism of the Holy Spirit, we must investigate how the early Christians received the Holy Spirit.

A Look at the Era of the Apostles

After the disciples saw Jesus Christ ascend into heaven from Mount Olivet, they obeyed Jesus' command and gathered together and earnestly prayed with one accord (see Acts 1:14).

Today, as much as in the past, those who want to receive the promised baptism of the Holy Spirit should have a fervent expectation and a desperate desire to receive.

During my gospel crusades, I have seen thousands of believers filled with the Holy Spirit. Almost without exception that

119

blessing has come when the seekers decided, regardless of circumstances or dignity, with tears of determination, that they would receive it without fail.

If those who want to receive the Holy Spirit are half in doubt about their own desire, if they pray with a lukewarm attitude that God will give them the baptism of the Holy Spirit if He wants to, they cannot receive no matter how long they pray. The blessing of the fullness of the Spirit of God always comes when you make up your mind that you will not leave without having the answer to your earnest, desperate need.

In Acts 8, the believers in Samaria received the Holy Spirit when Peter and John laid their hands on them.

The same experience happened to Saul (Paul), who received the Holy Spirit when Ananias laid hands on him (see Acts 9:10-18). A dozen believers in Ephesus also received the fullness of the Holy Spirit when hands were laid on them by the apostle Paul (see Acts 19:1-7).

Today also, it is well-known that you can receive the fullness of the Holy Spirit when hands are laid on you with prayer.

Of course, you cannot receive the Holy Spirit if hands are laid on you when you don't want to receive the baptism of the Holy Spirit or when your heart is not prepared or when you don't have a fervent faith to receive.

On the other hand, if the hands of Spirit-filled servants of God are laid on you, you can receive the fullness of the Holy Spirit when you have a strong desire to receive, even if your own prayer is weak.

Finally Acts 10:44-48 records the Spirit's filling the Gentiles at Cornelius's house. Verse 44 says, "While Peter yet spake these words, the Holy Ghost fell on them which heard the word."

These people were all filled with the Holy Spirit while they listened to Peter's preaching.

I have seen this happen. While preaching a sermon about the Holy Spirit, I've seen the Holy Spirit Himself poured out like rain upon prepared hearts. They spoke with tongues, magnifying God in a heavenly language, as believers did in the house of Cornelius.

From many pulpits today the true word of God is not preached faithfully. How can people hear the Word if it is not preached? Though people have worshipped in the church, they do not experience a deep moving or the wonderful grace of the Holy Spirit.

When a servant of the Lord, filled with the Spirit, preaches the anointed Word, listeners will experience a great moving of the Holy Spirit.

Preparing Our Hearts

How do we prepare our hearts to receive the baptism of the Holy Spirit?

First of all, those who want to receive the Holy Spirit should have not only a desire but also a knowledge of and grip on the trustworthy promises of God: He is still giving the same fullness of the Holy Spirit as He did in the era of the apostles. The Scripture concludes: "But let him ask in faith, nothing wavering. For he that wavereth is like a wave of the sea driven with the wind and tossed. For let not that man think that he shall receive any thing of the Lord. A double minded man is unstable in all his ways" (James 1:6-8).

If you seek to receive the Holy Spirit with an attitude of doubt, not fully trusting the promises of God, you are wasting your time and effort.

The Bible teaches us, "So then faith cometh by hearing, and hearing by the word of God" (Rom. 10:17). We should begin studying the book of Acts with a wide open heart, listening to the testimonies of those who have received the fullness of the Holy Spirit; we should remove all human prejudice from our hearts.

After we have the conviction that the blessing of the fullness of the Holy Spirit is for us today, we should repent of all unconfessed sins before God and depend upon the precious blood of Christ for a complete cleansing. We must take care of any sin in our lives before we pray for the experience of the baptism of the Spirit.

Peter said in Acts 2:38, "Repent, and be baptized every one of you in the name of Jesus Christ for the remission of sins, and ye shall receive the gift of the Holy Ghost."

Does this command, "Repent, and be baptized every one of you in the name of Jesus Christ for the remission of sins," mean that unless you are baptized with water you will receive neither remission of sins nor the Holy Spirit?

It seems not, as, when Peter preached the gospel in the house of Cornelius, Gentiles were filled with the Holy Spirit even before they had gone through the process of water baptism.

Needless to say, God cannot give the baptism of the Holy Spirit to those who have not received remission of sins or salvation.

When we repent and believe in the gospel, we receive remission of sins and salvation. We should also try to be baptized with water as soon as possible as it is the external sign of salvation. But to conclude that unless you are baptized with water, you receive neither remission of sins nor baptism of the Holy Spirit is against the teachings of the Bible.

I have seen tens of thousands of people repent and believe in the Lord Jesus Christ as Savior and then be filled with the Holy Spirit before they were baptized with water.

In Acts 10:48, the apostle Peter spoke to Gentiles who had received not only the forgiveness of sins but the fullness of the Holy Spirit and told them, "Be baptized in the name of the Lord."

Most of the believers who lived in the days of the apostles were exhorted to (and did) receive the Holy Spirit as soon as they were saved. But today a great number of believers "have not so much as heard whether there be any Holy Ghost" (Acts 19:2). What a sad commentary.

So though water baptism isn't a prerequisite for baptism with the Spirit, repentance is, because the Holy Spirit will not come to a vessel that conceals sin.

When we pray to receive the baptism of the Holy Spirit, there are generally two kinds of sins we should repent of: Have we knowingly disobeyed the will of God? Have we neglected the duty of believers—believing God's Word concerning being filled with the Holy Spirit?

The first sin is that of disobedience. Before believing in the Lord Jesus, we revolted against God and committed many kinds of sins. When we repented and accepted Jesus Christ as Savior, we received remission of sins. However, through our long revolt, our hearts had become so hardened that we were not broken easily. Though we have received remission of sins and salvation, when we want to receive the fullness of the Holy Spirit, we must repent bitterly again, asking for His forgiveness and cleansing from our willfulness.

In order to be broken before the Lord and cleansed, we should repent of all the transgressions we can remember.

I remember weeping continually for two years every time I prayed to receive the fullness of the Holy Spirit. Though I cried and prayed hard, I could not receive the baptism. At first I was very thirsty but later I grew disappointed and frustrated.

THE HOLY SPIRIT, MY SENIOR PARTNER

Then when I was in the second year of Bible school, I prayed with a resolute determination that I wouldn't leave the place where I was sitting until I had received the Holy Spirit. At the same time I confessed deeply once again all the sins I had committed since childhood. Suddenly my spirit was broken and the Holy Spirit of God moved upon me and within me with a great infilling. I began to speak with other tongues as the Holy Spirit gave me utterances.

The second sin we must confess is callousness. James 4:17 says, "Therefore to him that knoweth to do good, and doeth it not, to him it is sin." Though we are saved and live as Christians, if we have been lazy we should repent of the sin of laziness. We should repent that we have not lived with God at the center of our lives. If we have not sought the kingdom and His righteousness first, we have not pleased God.

When we repent of all our sins, the power of those sins will be broken. As we pray for the fullness of the Holy Spirit, we will have the right relationship with God—an obedient heart to do God's will.

As far as we have the ability, we need to make amends and repay what we owe to others. We need to ask their forgiveness and make restitution. Unlike repentance in word only, repentance and confession that come out of the inner heart are followed by the fruit of action.

When our hearts have been thus prepared, the Holy Spirit of God always comes down upon us.

Frequently, those who desire to receive the Holy Spirit after hearing someone's moving testimony make up their minds that they will receive the Holy Spirit in just the same manner. But the Holy Spirit does not always come down in accordance with the way we ask. He comes in accordance with the personality of the receiving person. Sometimes He comes calmly like soft rain. At other times He comes tumultuously like rolling thunder. Though the Holy Spirit makes Himself known in different ways, He who comes is still the same—the third person of the trinity.

A Word of Warning

After we have confessed sin, how should we pray to receive the Holy Spirit? Let me present a few observations or warnings in this regard.

First, we should not pray to receive the Holy Spirit with a wrong motive. In plain words, you must not cry to God so you can boast or gloat in the special attention that might accompany a great power. People who've asked amiss have sometimes received a different spirit, such as the spirit of covetousness, rather than the Holy Spirit.

But when the motivation of our hearts is pure—when we want to become a more powerful and effective vessel to be used by God, when we want to become by any means a better instrument of God, bearing witness of a Christlike spirit—evil spirits can never come near us.

Jesus spoke of such an assurance in Luke 11:11-13:

> If a son shall ask bread of any of you that is a father, will he give him a stone? or if he ask a fish, will he for a fish give him a serpent? Or if he shall ask an egg, will he offer him a scorpion? If ye then, being evil, know how to give good gifts unto your children: how much more shall your heavenly Father give the Holy Spirit to them that ask him?

Therefore when we pray for the fullness of the Holy Spirit so that the will of God for our lives may be fulfilled (not to satisfy our lust or covetousness), God will surely give us the Holy Spirit.

125

THE HOLY SPIRIT, MY SENIOR PARTNER

This second word of warning does not apply to a person who has a cheerful disposition but to the kind of person who is pessimistic and inclined to keep a dark solitude in his or her heart. Since this type of person has been so long oppressed unwittingly by a negative spirit, if he tries to pray hastily for the Spirit of God without first completely cleansing himself of that negative spirit, he can fall into agony and be overtaken by another morbid spirit.

But if this type of person has prepared himself slowly until his inner world, through receiving the Word of God and forgiveness in his heart, has become bright and cheerful and positive, he will receive a wonderful baptism.

When such a person comes to have a cheerful and positive mental attitude, he has already overcome and rid himself of the devil. He can pray for the fullness of the Holy Spirit without anxiety.

Third, a long continuing sickness which wears away the body is often followed by the oppression of the devil. Those who are weak both in mind and body, having been harassed by sickness a long time, should be cleansed by the precious blood of Jesus again; if they are inclined to be oppressed by the devil, when they pray earnestly to receive the Holy Spirit, they could be oppressed again by the devil.

Acts 10:38 teaches that during His ministry Jesus healed all diseases and sickness caused by the oppression of the devil: "God anointed Jesus of Nazareth with the Holy Ghost and with power: who went about doing good, and healing all that were oppressed of the devil; for God was with him."

I have almost always been hindered by the devil when I prayed with those weak in mind and body to receive the Holy Spirit. Knowing this, people who have been oppressed by Satan should pray to receive the Holy Spirit laying special claim to the precious blood of Jesus.

Fourth, those persons who served the devil long before they came to the Lord should be especially careful. Before these people pray to receive the Holy Spirit, they should bury all the past relationships they had with the devil, repent of their sins fully and have the victory all believers can have over the devil. Then when they pray to receive the Holy Spirit, they can pray for peace and the joy of Christ without any fear and sense of demonic oppression. Occasionally, these people may still be vulnerable subconsciously if they open their hearts.

Fifth, those who pray eagerly to receive the Holy Spirit should not permit just anyone to lay hands on them in prayer. An evil spirit, like an epidemic, is very contagious. I have seen numerous people taken by unclean spirits when someone with evil spirits laid hands on them. When they were seized by that spirit they experienced terrible suffering until they received deliverance. Those who want to have hands laid on them in prayer should always be sure that the person who is going to lay hands on them is a person full of the Spirit of truth.

Sixth, be wary of going alone to a mountain or a cave for prayer. Once in a while those who have heard of other people receiving much grace at a prayer mountain want to visit that place also. But then because their faith was not bold they became frightened and oppressed by evil spirits who took advantage of their moment of fear.

Throughout my ministry, as I have preached about the Holy Spirit, I have seen countless examples of what I've described in this section. Because of my experience, I have received considerable knowledge about how to free people from the bondage of the devil.

Now let us examine how to discriminate between the Holy Spirit and evil spirits.

8

Discerning Evil Spirits in a Person

Two spiritual forces surround us. Because of Jesus' great love for His redeemed ones, He has sent the Holy Spirit and many angels commanding them "to minister for them who shall be heirs of salvation" (Heb. 1:14).

Not only is the Holy Spirit with us always, but many angels are also with us always. On the other hand, the enemy, Satan, who is the prince of the power of the air, is continually devising a sinister plot "to steal, and to kill, and to destroy" by sending evil and unclean spirits who walk around in the world (John 10:10). As the apostle John says, "And we know that we are of God, and the whole world lieth in wickedness" (1 John 5:19).

Seeing that these facts are true, I have come to realize that believers should discern these spirits. If you don't have the special gift of discerning the spirits, discern the work of evil spirits by following the teaching of Christ.

Knowing a Tree by Its Fruit

Jesus teaches in Matthew 7:15-20:

> Beware of false prophets, which come to you in sheep's clothing, but inwardly they are ravening wolves. Ye shall know them by their fruits. Do men gather grapes of thorns, or figs of thistles? Even so every good tree bringeth forth good fruit; but a corrupt tree bringeth forth evil fruit. A good tree cannot bring forth evil fruit, neither can a corrupt tree bring forth good fruit. Every tree that bringeth not forth good fruit is hewn down, and cast into the fire. Wherefore by their fruits ye shall know them.

Even though you may have a fantastically wonderful experience or inspiration, if the fruit you bear is not in line with the Word of God and the fruit of the Holy Spirit, it can never be work that was born of the Spirit of God.

Jesus also warns:

> Many will say to me in that day, Lord, Lord, have we not prophesied in thy name? and in thy name have cast out devils? and in thy name done many wonderful works? And then will I profess unto them, I never knew you: depart from me, ye that work iniquity (Matt. 7:22,23).

You should never assume merely on the basis of its supernatural aspects that any work that is followed by signs and wonders is performed as the work of God. You should always look at the fruit of or the true nature behind the work. Though the devil comes in sheep's clothing, he can neither hide nor falsify his character. Let us examine the fruits of the devil.

The Devil Is Wicked

The Bible teaches that "the kingdom of God is...righteousness, and peace, and joy in the Holy Ghost" (Rom. 14:17). But when Satan comes in, disguised as the Holy Spirit, he steals away a person's love, joy and peace.

James 3:14-18 gives us a clear standard of judgment:

> But if ye have bitter envying and strife in your hearts, glory not, and lie not against the truth. This wisdom descendeth not from above, but is earthly, sensual, devilish. For where envying and strife is, there is confusion and every evil work. But the wisdom that is from above is first pure, then peaceable, gentle, and easy to be intreated, full of mercy and good fruits, without partiality, and without hypocrisy. And the fruit of righteousness is sown in peace of them that make peace.

Those who are depressed by the spirit of the devil feel a strong interference in everything. It can be so great that the person begins to wonder, If this is the Holy Spirit, how can He act so frivolously and prompt such thoughtless action?

At times, the spirit of the devil tries to give instructions that imitate pretty well the Holy Spirit. These are not only about petty things but also about problems of faith. The evil spirits also spread negativism and anxiety. In short, evil spirits continue unceasingly to send troublesome prophetic interference.

Clear words in Isaiah teach us about being associated with familiar spirits: "And when they shall say unto you, Seek unto them that have familiar spirits, and unto wizards that peep, and that mutter: should not a people seek unto their God? for the living to the dead?'' (Is. 8:19).

Believers who go around making jabbering and muttering prophecies probably have familiar spirits, and they should be stopped.

Prophecy from the Holy Spirit comes as God needs to speak His message to His people. It comes gently and is divinely accompanied by deep feelings of confirmation and assurance that the message was truly from God.

The Devil Is Unclean

In many places, the Bible calls spirits ''unclean'' (see Matt. 10:1; Mark 1:27; Luke 6:18). Unclean spirits, the spirit of the devil, raise ugly imaginations continually against one's own will. They stick like a bur in one's heart, unlike an occasional passing thought. Sometimes unclean spirits cause people to have bad thoughts when they read the Bible. Sometimes they make one feel sick when in the presence of Spirit-filled believers. Those who are oppressed by unclean spirits are in agony, with lewd and filthy imaginations overflowing like a cesspool. When they hear the Word of God, uncontrollable false charges will afflict their hearts and arrogant thinking will rise as a snake raises its head.

Luke 6:18 says that these unclean spirits can ''vex.'' The Holy Spirit of God brings joy, peace and a refreshing, but evil spirits bring agony and trouble to mind and body.

Though you may believe that you have received the Holy Spirit, if you are in continual agony, fear and trouble, if you always feel pressed down by a big burden, this is the sign that you are oppressed by evil spirits.

No matter how deceitfully the devil may disguise himself, when you see such fruit, you can know that his true character is like a ravening wolf.

Discerning a Person's Concept of Christ

The most important question in discerning spirits is, What does one say about Christ?

Other discrepancies in doctrine do not reach the point of life and death. But false teaching about the saving grace of Jesus Christ brings eternal destruction to those who preach it and those who hear and follow it.

The apostle John writes in 1 John 4:1-3:

> Beloved, believe not every spirit, but try the spirits whether they are of God: because many false prophets are gone out into the world. Hereby know ye the Spirit of God: Every spirit that confesseth that Jesus Christ is come in the flesh is of God: And every spirit that confesseth not that Jesus Christ is come in the flesh is not of God: and this is that spirit of antichrist, whereof ye have heard that it should come; and even now already is it in the world.

Though someone insists that he has received the fullness of the Holy Spirit, though someone prophesies wonderful things and does mighty acts, if he does not claim that Jesus Christ was born of a virgin and was crucified for the redemption of the whole world, he is not of Christ. If he does not claim that Jesus Christ rose from the grave on the third day, that He ascended into heaven and sits at the right hand of the throne of God, that He will come down in the same appearance as He was resurrected in the flesh, he does not teach by the Holy Spirit but by the spirit of antichrist.

Considering this, in many countries countless religious groups lead a great many people to destruction with completely false doctrines about Christ.

As familiar examples, a person may insist that he is "the

133

Christ'' and another may argue that he is "the only Lamb,'' threatening that unless people follow him, they are not saved. Others may contend that there is no need for Jesus to be our mediator because one can communicate directly with the Father. Because there is such a chaotic spirit in the world, we must "believe not every spirit," but strictly "try the spirits whether they are of God."

When I see believers who have latched onto a self-appointed man of grace who shows mysterious power, unconditionally following him and throwing their souls before him, I cannot help but sigh. They have not been cautious enough.

Discerning a Person's Words

A person's speech transmits character and thought. An angry woman uses angry language. A coarse man uses vulgar language. A merciful man uses merciful language, and a good woman uses good language.

The Bible also teaches this clearly: "No man speaking by the Spirit of God calleth Jesus accursed: and no man can say that Jesus is the Lord, but by the Holy Ghost" (1 Cor. 12:3).

Therefore, when we hear a person claim to have received grace, we should listen discreetly and carefully. To discern a person's spirit, for what should we listen?

No Praise to Self

When a person who claims to have received the Holy Spirit praises himself whenever possible instead of giving glory to Jesus, he does not speak by the Spirit of Christ; he speaks by the spirit of covetousness.

The devil always shakes and rages like a serpent ready to strike, and all in an effort to show off. If a person's talk honors self instead of Christ, the words are of a spirit of evil, not the Holy Spirit.

Sometimes a person who professes to have received a lot of grace will come to me and say, "Pastor, I have received much grace. The Holy Spirit told me that He loves me particularly and that He will make me a great servant by using me mightily...." If I keep listening, I often grow disgusted, because that person is not speaking words to honor Christ and God; the words are merely self-praise.

The Holy Spirit magnifies God (see Acts 10:46) and reveals the glory of Christ through us by filling us and showing us what He received of Christ (see John 16:1-14).

Whether talking privately or speaking publicly, if a person, even a servant of the Lord, shows off his own greatness, not Christ's, he is already taken by the spirit of antichrist.

No Threatening or Hurting Others
When a person who professes to have received the Holy Spirit does nothing but threaten and blackmail others, when he doesn't hesitate to use coarse and hurtful language, we must be careful.

A certain sister who professed that she had received the Holy Spirit carried with her a cloud of terror instead of love and peace. If anyone corrected her, she would call down a curse. How can the personality of the Holy Spirit of God which is meek and humble dwell in the life of one who speaks such words?

How can that kind of person (claiming to be speaking by the Holy Spirit and favored with special blessing) knock on believers' doors, whisper slander to church members and demand hush money unscrupulously?

A Word of Warning
Before we affirm what wonderful works a person does, we

must first notice if he or she praises God and preaches Christ as the Lord. We must see evidence of humility, of a person hidden behind the cross, speaking and acting out the fruit of the Holy Spirit.

The apostle Paul warns us about believers in the latter times: "Now the Spirit speaketh expressly, that in the latter times some shall depart from the faith, giving heed to seducing spirits, and doctrines of devils" (1 Tim. 4:1).

Wherever the real thing exists, there will be counterfeits. Therefore, we should not only always examine our own spiritual experience, but also look to discerning the spirits in order to guide our fellowship with other believers.

9

Gifts of the Holy Spirit

First Corinthians 12:4-11 gives us a classification of the gifts of the Spirit:

Now there are diversities of gifts, but the same Spirit. And there are differences of administrations, but the same Lord. And there are diversities of operations, but it is the same God which worketh all in all. But the manifestation of the Spirit is given to every man to profit withal. For to one is given by the Spirit the word of wisdom; to another the word of knowledge by the same Spirit; to another faith by the same Spirit; to another the gifts of healing by the same Spirit; to another the working of miracles; to another prophecy; to another discerning of spirits; to another divers kinds of tongues;

to another the interpretation of tongues; but all these worketh that one and the selfsame Spirit, dividing to every man severally as he will.

The Gifts of God

Let's look at what Paul says: "There are diversities of operations, but it is the same God which worketh all in all" (1 Cor. 12:6).

This word *operation* refers to the *method* used to preach the gospel. To be more specific, it refers to the overall strategic operation used in taking or sending the gospel forth. Effective ways and policies for witnessing of the gospel include pioneering new churches, being used of God to bring revival, and establishing and maintaining schools and hospitals. All these belong to the diverse operations that God uses to further the gospel.

The Gifts of Jesus

Paul also says, "And there are differences of administrations, but the same Lord" (1 Cor. 12:5). This means that *Jesus Christ* has given the gift of administration to some believers to carry out important leadership and supportive roles within the church. As every organization on earth requires responsible leadership, so does the church, the body of Jesus Christ.

Administration is explained in several places in the Bible. One example, 1 Corinthians 12:27,28, reads, "Now ye are the body of Christ, and members in particular. And God hath set some in the church, first apostles, secondarily prophets, thirdly teachers, after that miracles, then gifts of healings, helps, governments, diversities of tongues."

Concerning this administration, Paul wrote in Ephesians 4:11, "And he [the Lord Jesus Christ] gave some, apostles; and some, prophets; and some, evangelists; and some, pastors and teachers." This verse shows that as believers we cannot choose the type of administration we would like to have within the church. Rather we should each find the gift of Jesus we have received and then serve God faithfully in that place of service.

The Gifts of the Spirit

Now, finally, gifts are given by the Holy Spirit: "Now there are diversities of gifts, but the same Spirit" (1 Cor. 12:4).

Gifts of the Holy Spirit are the means and instruments of power to carry out successfully the operation and administration of God's work in His church.

When a plan has been made to build a big house and the architect, builder and specialists have been appointed, then all the tools and materials needed to build the house are brought in and used so that the project is finished successfully as soon as possible.

When there is a great work to do for God, the gifts of the Holy Spirit are given to different believers within the church, His body. These enable believers to accomplish His work and responsibility effectively and the work grows because of the gifts of the Holy Spirit.

There are nine gifts of the Holy Spirit, and they can be divided roughly into the following three groups:

1. The gifts of revelation
    a. The gift of the word of wisdom
    b. The gift of the word of knowledge
    c. The gift of discerning of spirits
2. The vocal gifts
    a. The gift of tongues
    b. The gift of interpretation of tongues

   c. The gift of prophecy
3. The gifts of power
   a. The gift of faith
   b. The gift of healing
   c. The gift of working of miracles

The gifts of revelation deal with supernatural communication revealed through the Holy Spirit to the heart of one who has received this gift. The knowledge of other people's experiences and situations that is revealed through these gifts is not made known to the public until those who have received any or all of these gifts choose to speak.

The vocal gifts deal with supernatural communication that the Holy Spirit of God reveals by using the human voice. Not only the person using the gifts but others around him or her can hear these gifts and therefore they can be received by the senses.

The gifts of power are mighty gifts in which the power of God appears so as to manifest a miraculous answer through a supernatural, creative intervention. Through these gifts people and their environments are changed.

All of these gifts are distributed to people by the Holy Spirit in accordance with His own will for the benefit and growth of the church, the body of Christ.

The Manifestation of the Holy Spirit

Sometimes, believers who have received the fullness of the Holy Spirit and the accompanying gifts greatly misunderstand these manifestations of the Holy Spirit (see 1 Cor. 12:7).

Some people think that anyone who has received the fullness and various gifts of the Holy Spirit can use the gifts as he or she likes and whenever he or she likes.

For this reason, occasionally we see people who have supposedly received special favor or gifts from God try to use those gifts as if the Holy Spirit were a personal servant. This of course is extremely dangerous because the Holy Spirit in us is the third person of the holy three-in-one God.

When someone has this attitude, the Holy Spirit is grieved. When the Holy Spirit is grieved, the gifts will cease operating through such people. When they sense this in their spirits, these people usually become arrogant. In order to make others believe that the gifts still flow through them, they will operate in the flesh (which is fraud), often speaking lies, which brings disgrace to the church.

The gifts are the possession of the Holy Spirit Himself. Since they are His, they cannot exist independently apart from Him. The gifts of the Holy Spirit can by no means be used at a person's own will. Only the Holy Spirit can possess them absolutely and manifest them through believers in whom He abides.

The truth is not that man uses the gifts of the Holy Spirit. Rather the Holy Spirit, who occupies man and fills him, uses that person and manifests the gifts through him according to His own will, time and situation.

The apostle Paul wrote clearly about these instructions when he said, ''But the manifestation of the Spirit is given to every man to profit withal'' (1 Cor. 12:7).

Sometimes arrogant and haughty men have tried to use the Holy Spirit as though He were a clown in a circus. I have felt disillusioned and embarrassed when I have seen them being glorified. They seemed to have no idea that they were standing in the presence of God and the Holy Spirit.

I'm not saying that these people did not receive the gifts of the Holy Spirit. What I am saying is that they greatly misunderstood the purpose of the gifts in their lives. Because they had received certain gifts they thought they could use the Holy Spirit as they desired and when they desired. But the Holy Spirit fills believers to become vessels to manifest the gifts only so the hearers of the gospel will be edified.

What should be the proper attitude of a believer who has experienced the gifts of the Holy Spirit? He should humble himself continually before the presence of God, dedicate himself as a pure vessel and then wait for the Holy Spirit to manifest the gifts through him at a time and place He chooses.

If the Holy Spirit chooses to manifest diverse gifts through us, we should keep our hearts humble and depend utterly upon Him. This will open the way wider for Him to edify His church through His gifts, through us.

I have had the blessed experience of having diverse gifts operating through me, and I am still praying for even more manifestations of the Holy Spirit. The only reason I was able to build a church of five hundred thousand members in less than thirty years was because of the wonderful manifestation of the Holy Spirit flowing through the gifts of revelation, the vocal gifts or the gifts of power. As this happened we gave all the glory to God for what He was accomplishing.

Even to this day, one thing that makes me tremble with carefulness is the thought that I might resist the Holy Spirit or that when He does move through me—to manifest the many gifts to edify His church—I might be misunderstood to be speaking on my own.

In summary, the gifts belong absolutely to the Holy Spirit. The gifts and the Holy Spirit cannot be separated and the only purpose for the Holy Spirit manifesting diverse gifts through people is for the edification of His church.

How to Receive the Gifts

How can we become the vessel through which the Holy Spirit will manifest His gifts?

The Holy Spirit of God does not distinguish among persons as long as they have received the fullness of the Holy Spirit and manifest the gifts and edify believers. First Corinthians 12:7 reads, ''But the manifestation of the Spirit is given to *every man* to profit withal,'' to clarify that He will use anyone who has received the fullness of the Spirit as a vessel through which He will manifest the gifts.

To say that the Holy Spirit chooses us as the vessels through which He manifests the gifts is more correct than to say that we have received the gifts, for, as I've said, the distribution of the gifts is absolutely up to the will of the Holy Spirit. After listing the gifts Paul says, ''But all these worketh that one and the selfsame Spirit, dividing to every man severally as he will'' (1 Cor. 12:11).

If you covet the gifts, the proper prayer is not to specify your own desire for specific gifts. You should find which gifts the indwelling Holy Spirit desires to manifest through you according to *His* desire and will for the edification of the church.

Today's childhood educators try to find the nature and temperament of a child and then develop that temperament. In this same way you should observe carefully which gifts the Holy Spirit wants to manifest through you after you've received the fullness of the Holy Spirit. Once you know the gifts He has chosen and given to you, cultivate and develop them by allowing Him to manifest these gifts through you.

When I first received the Holy Spirit, I prayed blindly for more of the gift that was most popular, the gift of healing, for the gift of the word of wisdom and for the gift of the word of knowledge. Though I prayed at length with many tears, the

THE HOLY SPIRIT, MY SENIOR PARTNER

anticipated gifts were not forthcoming. Though it seemed that those gifts appeared for a while, I did not have an outstanding flow of those gifts of the Spirit continually. Instead, gifts I did not ask for or pay much attention to began to appear in my personal life and ministry like new shoots of grass sprouting on the earth.

The gifts I received were none other than the gift of faith and the gift of prophecy. In both my personal life and ministry, supernatural faith captured my heart as if some mysterious power like Samson's had been given to me. Bold confession which could command mountains to be moved into the sea sprang out from my mouth and the miracles actually happened as I spoke.

Those gifts did not stay with me continuously. The gift of faith does not manifest itself in every situation. When the will of the Holy Spirit was manifested for the glory of God, more faith than I could ever imagine in my situation sprang out of the depths of my heart. The same happened with the gift of prophecy. Frankly, I was never interested in prophecy. Because of the many undesirable results and confusion that some prophecies brought, I would rather have rebuked those who prophesied. To this day I believe the same; yet, out of the blue, the spirit of prophecy began to make my heart flutter with anticipation of His words. When the words of prophecy come, divine wisdom and comfort and direction fill my heart. Needless to say, we should never be boastful of these gifts nor show off indiscriminately.

It is proper that these gifts be used only as a means to prove the eternal, unchanging, infallible, perfect Word of God, not to show off a person's spirituality.

As I have said, once we find out our gift, given according to the Spirit of God, we must develop that gift, letting it manifest itself often. While our gift is blessing the church and God's people, it is also helping us grow and mature as Christians.

When the Holy Spirit wants to manifest some gifts through a person who is afraid to speak out or who, preferring to please other people, refuses to obey the prompting, the Holy Spirit is grieved and quenched. If this happens often, the gifts will disappear. Those who have learned which gift they have received should not be partial to people or organizations. Rather they should simply allow the Holy Spirit to be manifested through them so that those gifts will be permanent, appearing more often to bring blessing to the church and believers.

Also, those who have received the gifts should diligently search the Scriptures and study the circumstances in which the same gifts were used. This study should be accompanied by pruning one's life of wrongdoing.

The gifts can never take the place of the Word of God, our highest authority and our instruction for living. They should always be controlled by the Word of God and be in harmony with the Scriptures. They should be utilized within the boundaries laid down by God's Word.

Can a person possess diverse gifts at the same time?

Needless to say, Jesus used all nine gifts of the Spirit, and we are confident from the Scriptures that the apostles, such as Peter or Paul, also used all nine gifts. How can ordinary believers like you and me today receive all nine gifts?

The Bible states, "But covet earnestly the best gifts" (1 Cor. 12:31). Some people say that love is the best gift, but this understanding is not correct.

First Corinthians 13 says that love is the best way to use the gifts. The Scripture "But covet earnestly the best gifts: and yet shew I unto you a more excellent way" means that the Bible is showing us *the way* to use the gifts. First Corinthians 14:12

also reads, "Even so ye, forasmuch as ye are zealous of spiritual gifts, seek that ye may *excel to the edifying of the church*" (italics mine).

These Scripture passages show that God wants to use to the utmost believers who have received the fullness of the Holy Spirit. When Paul says we should covet the best gifts, he means this: When we desire earnestly that the gifts already being used would be used more, then God, in accordance with His holy will, will give us greater and more abundant gifts. From this we can conclude that Christians can surely possess various gifts at the same time. The gifts of the Spirit are His to give as He wills.

10

The Gifts of Revelation

The Gift of the Word of Knowledge

The Bible refers to this gift as "the word of knowledge" (1 Cor. 12:8) instead of the gift of "knowledge" and there is a reason for this distinction. If we were to refer to this gift as the gift of knowledge, it would include all of the knowledge concerning God. But the gift of the word of knowledge refers only to a portion of God's knowledge that God wants to reveal.

Knowledge refers to the condition of knowing something through realization of truth concerning things and matters; today, however, many people greatly misunderstand the gift of the word of knowledge.

Some people act and speak as if they were a walking

dictionary because they have received the gift of the word of knowledge, but actually their behavior itself shows that they are very ignorant. Though they have received this gift, it does not mean that they have received the whole knowledge of the omniscient and omnipotent God.

Other people say that they have received the gift of the word of knowledge because their taste for learning has led them to study deeply the Word of God. Because of this, they say, they have received the gift of the word of knowledge.

But the gift of the word of knowledge manifested as one of the gifts of the Holy Spirit is not the knowledge that can be studied and learned. It cannot be investigated or accumulated either. This knowledge, which reveals the hidden truth of things and matters and solves problems at a certain time and place for the glory of God according to His special revelation, comes only by the inspiration of the Holy Spirit.

The manifestation of this kind of knowledge does not mean that one possesses the whole knowledge of omniscient God or has acquired knowledge as a result of research. The word of knowledge is information revealed to one who has this gift when a special need for the kingdom of God and the cause of the gospel of Christ must be uncovered or revealed to the children of God. When there is no human way for us to know the circumstances, God reveals this partial knowledge to believers through the Holy Spirit by revelation, dreams or visions. This means that the knowledge, given in a supernatural way by the revelation of God, is not gained through human means or efforts.

The Scriptures give us many instances where the gift of the word of knowledge operated supernaturally through God's people by the Holy Spirit.

Let's review some of these instances.

In Joshua 7 after conquering the strong city of Jericho, the children of Israel tried to invade a much smaller city of Ai but were defeated miserably.

At that time, Joshua rent his clothes and fell on his face. With the elders of Israel before the ark of the Lord, he put dust upon his head and prayed. As a result, in the evening the revelation of God came to the children of Israel: Because one person had stolen something in Jericho against the direct command of God not to touch anything, God's anger had been kindled; He was not with them when they attacked Ai.

Joshua received this word of knowledge—the reason why the children of Israel were defeated before their enemy. More than this, through the revelation of the Holy Spirit, Joshua received information that the man who committed the sin was Achan, the son of Carmi, the son of Zabdi, the son of Zerah, of the tribe of Judah.

Such knowledge is neither received by an effort of human study nor by the information secretly transmitted from one person to another. It is only the knowledge that the Holy Spirit reveals to those who have received this gift.

In 1 Samuel 9 there is another scene: Saul and those who were with him went out to search for the lost donkeys of Saul's father. When they couldn't find them, they came near to the seer Samuel to inquire. When Samuel met Saul, Samuel said immediately, "And as for thine asses that were lost three days ago, set not thy mind on them; for they are found" (1 Sam. 9:20).

Even before Samuel talked with Saul, Samuel knew not only that Saul was searching for the asses, but that they had already been found. Such a revelation came by the gift of the word of knowledge.

The gift of the word of knowledge worked greatly in the life of Elisha in 2 Kings 6:8-12:

> Then the king of Syria warred against Israel, and took counsel with his servants, saying, In such and such a place shall be my camp. And the man of God sent unto the king of Israel, saying, Beware that thou pass not such a place; for thither the Syrians are come down.... Therefore the heart of the king of Syria was sore troubled for this thing; and he called his servants, and said unto them, Will ye not shew me which of us is for the king of Israel? And one of his servants said, None, my Lord, O king: but Elisha, the prophet that is in Israel, telleth the king of Israel the words that thou speakest in thy bedchamber.

Such wonderful knowledge was not obtained by an intelligence network of men, but what God revealed in person to Elisha through the gift of the Holy Spirit.

The gift of the word of knowledge was wonderfully manifested also to the believers of the New Testament. The case of our Lord Jesus Christ goes without saying. So let us look into the experience of the apostle Peter.

In Acts 5 Ananias and his wife, Sapphira, consulted together and sold their possessions. They brought a certain part of the proceeds and laid it at the apostles' feet—as if it were the whole price. They were convinced that no one knew about their lie.

But Peter said, "Ananias, why hath Satan filled thine heart to lie to the Holy Ghost, and to keep back part of the price of the land? While it remained, was it not thine own? and after it was sold, was it not in thine power? why hast thou conceived this thing in thine heart? thou hast not lied unto men, but unto God" (Acts 5:3,4). God had told Peter what he needed to know in a situation.

I, too, have had similar experiences. One Christmas morning, following the all-night prayer meeting, I led an early morning service at the church. My schedule was heavy and I was going to go home to sleep a little before I led the regular eleven o'clock service.

When I came back home, I was hungry. I was about to eat breakfast when suddenly there came to my mind an instruction: I was to go immediately to the church; something had happened. In my heart, I didn't want to move my body, but as a servant of the Lord I couldn't help obeying. So I got up right away and went to the church.

In the church everything was quiet. It seemed that nothing had happened. I met only a young janitor hired by the church who was sweeping the trash littered by believers who had attended the all-night prayer meeting.

I couldn't find anything to confirm the Holy Spirit's word to me that something had happened in the church. I craned my neck to check inside the sanctuary. Suddenly there came to my heart a further instruction: I was to go over to the platform. I walked to the platform and searched the pulpit, and there lay a tightly sealed big envelope containing an offering.

I took it in my hand and looked carefully at the sealed part. Thinking that I would return home after I warmed myself a little, I went to the office where there was a stove. With the envelope in my hand, I pulled up a chair near the stove.

Suddenly there was a loud knock on the door. I said, "Come in," and the young man who had been sweeping entered the office. His face was pale and he knelt down on the floor. To my great surprise he said, "Pastor, today I have come to know that God truly lives. I have committed a terrible crime, but please forgive me."

I was so dumbfounded I couldn't understand what he was

saying, but the young janitor kept his eyes downward and continued: "When I was sweeping the inside of the church, I found that big envelope of money on the platform. I looked around, no one was in the church at the moment, and I became covetous of it.

"I took the envelope and ran to my room and opened it with a razor. I took out some money. After putting back the remainder, I pasted it well and put it back on the pulpit before anyone would know. Everything was just as it had been, and I was sure that no one would ever notice. Then, though you had gone home to sleep, you suddenly appeared, nervously looking around to find something. Reassuring myself that you, a human being, couldn't possibly know anything of this, I kept on sweeping the floor.

"I felt uneasy, so I kept looking inside the church to see what you were doing. Then, just as I feared, you stepped on the platform, took the envelope of money, examined the sealed part and went to the office.

"I knew that all these things were revealed to you by the Holy Spirit, and I was so pricked in my conscience that I came here to confess my sin. Please forgive me."

Hearing the confession of that young man, I shuddered at the thought that I also am so closely searched by the Holy Spirit, who is always with us.

Another incident like this happened to a friend of mine some years ago near the end of the Korean Democratic Party administration. Mr. Bethel, an American missionary I was well acquainted with, moved from the Philippines to Korea for mission work. He and his family came to Korea by plane after sending his household effects securely by ship.

When his goods arrived, he received a consignment list from the Pusan Pier Custom House. He went there to get his belongings, but some of their most valuable things were nowhere to be found. They were included on the consignment list, and everything had been shipped at the same time, yet he was told that these certain items had not arrived at Korea.

Mr. Bethel was very annoyed and kept on asking questions until at last some customs officials grew angry and yelled at him.

Feeling depressed and mistreated, Mr. Bethel prayed to God earnestly right then and there and in a sudden vision he saw the inside of a warehouse with a small door. It was out of sight but just several feet to the left side of where he stood. Inside the door were hidden his valuable things.

Mr. Bethel asked customs officials to allow him to search in person and they triumphantly said, "OK."

Mr. Bethel walked straight ahead as he had seen in his vision and, sure enough, there was a hidden hallway. When he turned down that hall, he saw a small door as he had seen in the vision. When he approached the door, the faces of the customs officials turned red. They told him he could not go in that room, but he pushed them aside, opened the door and there were all his things, hidden just as it had been revealed to him.

The Holy Spirit of God gave Mr. Bethel the necessary knowledge for the moment, and through that supernatural gift of the word of knowledge he was able to solve the problem at hand.

Such a gift of the word of knowledge is never the kind of knowledge that man can possess on his own and use as freely as water, but the Holy Spirit of God possesses it and through the vessel of His choosing He manifests it as it is needed. He shows the glory of God and solves the problem.

The Gift of the Word of Wisdom

A person may be very learned and may have a lot of

knowledge, but unless that person has wisdom, he can't use that knowledge.

Wisdom is the function by which we can effectively use knowledge—to solve problems and bring forth blessings and victory. Even if someone has only a small bit of knowledge, if he is equipped with a great amount of wisdom, he can magnify greatly the knowledge he has. On the contrary, if someone has much knowledge, but lacks in wisdom, his knowledge can become buried knowledge which may never be fully known.

Then what is the gift of the word of wisdom?

The gift of the word of wisdom does not refer to any human wisdom. Those who don't understand this sometimes speak of believers who are especially bright and intelligent as people who have received the gift of wisdom, but this is wrong.

The word of wisdom referred to as a gift of the Holy Spirit (see 1 Cor. 12:8) is given only supernaturally to a believer who through this wisdom wonderfully solves problems in difficult circumstances and thereby gives glory to God.

The Bible urges that those who lack wisdom should ask such wisdom of God. "If any of you lack wisdom, let him ask of God, that giveth to all men liberally, and upbraideth not; and it shall be given him" (James 1:5).

In the Old Testament we can find the scene in which God manifested wisdom through King Solomon, the son of David. For example, let us read the incident written in 1 Kings 3:16-28:

> Then came there two women, that were harlots, unto the king, and stood before him. And the one woman said, O my lord, I and this woman dwell in one house; and I was delivered of a child with her in the house. And it came to pass the third day after that I was delivered, that this woman was delivered also: and we were together; there was no stranger with us in the

house, save we two in the house. And this woman's child died in the night; because she overlaid it. And she arose at midnight, and took my son from beside me, while thine handmaid slept, and laid it in her bosom, and laid her dead child in my bosom. And when I rose in the morning to give my child suck, behold, it was dead: but when I had considered it in the morning, behold, it was not my son, which I did bear. And the other woman said, Nay; but the living is my son, and the dead is thy son. And this said, No; but the dead is thy son, and the living is my son. Thus they spake before the king. Then said the king, The one saith, This is my son that liveth, and thy son is the dead: and the other saith, Nay; but thy son is the dead, and my son is the living. And the king said, Bring me a sword. And they brought a sword before the king. And the king said, Divide the living child in two, and give half to the one, and half to the other. Then spake the woman whose the living child was unto the king, for her bowels yearned upon her son, and she said, O my lord, give her the living child, and in no wise slay it. But the other said, Let it be neither mine nor thine, but divide it. Then the king answered and said, Give her the living child, and in no wise slay it: she is the mother thereof. And all Israel heard of the judgment which the king had judged; and they feared the king: for they saw that the wisdom of God was in him, to do judgment.

The exact wisdom in this passage was not a natural gift with which Solomon was born. "The wisdom of God was in him" expresses the gift God manifested for the need of that time through the power of the Holy Spirit, which was given to him by God.

THE HOLY SPIRIT, MY SENIOR PARTNER

The Bible calls it the gift of "the word of wisdom" instead of the gift of "wisdom," which would have meant that all-round wisdom given at all times, but the Bible teaches that it is the *gift* of the word of wisdom. In contrast to the all-round wisdom which humans can use freely as they want, God manifests the word of wisdom in accordance with a specific need and in a time and place for the glory of God and the power of the gospel. God speaks to us in this same manner. Though He is always with us, He does not speak at all times but speaks only in case of need.

In the expression, "I have received the gift of the word of wisdom," we should always put our emphasis on that part: "the word."

The manifestation of the gift of the word of wisdom is wonderfully clear in the life of Jesus. In Matthew 22:15-22, the story goes like this. The Pharisees were sure they had a way to entangle Jesus. In the presence of some Romans they asked Him if it was lawful for a Jew to give tribute to Caesar. If Jesus answered they should give tribute to Caesar, they were going to pounce upon Him, judging that He was a tool of Rome and the enemy of the Jewish people. But if He answered that they should not give tribute to Caesar, the Roman governor would charge Him with treason and send Him to prison.

They were confident of their trick, but they were dumbfounded by the words of wisdom with which He answered them.

Jesus told them to show Him a coin and, pointing to the image inscribed on it, He asked whose image it was.

When they said, "Caesar's," He answered, "Render therefore unto Caesar the things which are Caesar's; and unto God the things that are God's." Jesus gave them an answer which couldn't be caught by any noose. It was a word of wisdom, spoken by the power of the Spirit to address the matter at hand.

This happened again when the scribes and Pharisees were tempting Jesus. They brought Him a woman taken in adultery: "Master, this woman was taken in adultery, in the very act. Now Moses in the law commanded us, that such should be stoned: but what sayest thou?" (John 8:4,5).

They invented another trick, hoping to trap Jesus. If Jesus said that the woman should be stoned, they would accuse Him of acting against the law of love that He preached and that His miracles portrayed. But if Jesus opposed the punishment that Moses plainly commanded, they would drag Him off to their court.

How did Jesus answer? Jesus said, "He that is without sin among you, let him first cast a stone at her" (John 8:7). However hardened they might have been, they couldn't help but be pricked in their hearts before this sharp word of wisdom. John says, "They which heard it, being convicted by their own conscience, went out one by one, beginning at the eldest, even unto the last: and Jesus was left alone, and the woman standing in the midst" (John 8:9).

When we see Jesus solving such difficult problems one after another by a word of wisdom, we cannot help but be overwhelmed with respect and love.

Since this same Lord is our living Savior, no matter what difficulty we are confronted with, we should look to Him and not be discouraged.

God has promised to give us such a word of wisdom when we are persecuted for our faith in the Lord Jesus Christ and the gospel:

> But before all these, they shall lay their hands on you, and persecute you, delivering you up to the synagogues, and into prisons, being brought before kings and rulers for my name's sake. And it shall turn to you for a

testimony. Settle it therefore in your hearts, not to meditate before what ye shall answer: For I will give you a mouth and *wisdom*, which all your adversaries shall not be able to gainsay nor resist (Luke 21:12-15, italics mine).

These wonderful words "mouth and wisdom" mean that the gift of the word of wisdom will be given to us when the need arises. Here again, the promise is that such wisdom will not be given to us by nature. But when we meet an insurmountable barrier, God, by giving the wonderful wisdom of the Holy Spirit, will enable us easily to overcome the difficulty and solve the problem. Jesus' words mean that only the Holy Spirit possesses the gift and He manifests it from time to time through believers as the vessels.

The Gift of Discerning of Spirits

"...to another [is given] discerning of spirits" (1 Cor. 12:10).

Many people today confuse the gift of discerning of spirits with mind reading. Often those who profess to have received the gift of discerning of spirits create great disturbances in churches, volunteering to take the role of spiritual detective.

The gift is exactly what it says: the gift that is able to discern spirits. To put it simply, in this universe there are spirits belonging to God and spirits belonging to the devil; then there are instances when words are spoken by the spirit of man which is distinguished from the Holy Spirit or the spirit of Satan. We discern the spirits by the manifestation of the Holy Spirit, judging whether the spirit is from God or if someone is speaking by the spirit of man or by the spirit of Satan.

In 1 John 4:1, the apostle John wrote of the importance of discerning of spirits: "Beloved, believe not every spirit, but try the spirits whether they are of God: because many false prophets are gone out into the world.''

In these last days, unless you have the gift of discerning of spirits, you are exposed to the danger of being seduced. The apostle Paul said in 1 Timothy 4:1, ''Now the Spirit speaketh expressly that in the latter days some shall depart from the faith, giving heed to seducing spirits, and doctrines of devils.''

Unless we are quickly able to discern and oppose those who enter our midst with seducing spirits and doctrines of devils, great harm will come to the flock of weak believers.

Like any other gift, the gift of discerning of spirits is not that which anyone can possess and use freely at any time. This gift is in the hand of the Holy Spirit and He manifests it according to His need through the vessel God chooses.

Through my ministry, I have experienced the manifestation of this gift many times which became opportunities to set the church straight.

Once, a member of my congregation professed that she had received the wonderful gift of prophecy; in fact her prophecies came true several times.

As a result, many weak believers were so carried away by her prophecies that they set aside the practice of personal prayer, Scripture reading and the life of faith. Their guide was this prophecy. They flocked to this woman to hear the so-called message of God about the problems of their daily lives as they might consult a fortune-teller.

Since I could not immediately discern whether this was from God or from the devil, I watched as a spectator for a while. But with the passing of time it became clear that the fruit of the woman was not the fruit of the Holy Spirit. The attitude of her prophecy was not only fickle and frivolous; it had no meekness, love and peace like a dove. Rather her words were cold and fearful and destructive.

When I hinted that the spirit of the woman might not be of the Holy Spirit, not only the woman herself but many of her followers resisted and defied me. They said that a servant of the Lord motivated by jealousy was plotting to injure her.

I was in an awkward situation and became slightly bewildered. What if the woman really were speaking by the Holy Spirit? I didn't want to fall into the sin of resisting the Holy Spirit.

I threw myself down before God and prayed that He would reveal the truth to me by manifesting the gift of discerning of spirits. In a vision, He showed me that the spirit in her was an unclean spirit.

With this discernment, I had courage to discipline her with conviction. As a result, the church was delivered when it was just on the verge of a tempest. Peace was restored.

Nowadays, in the Korean churches people are eager to beguile with seducing spirits and doctrines of devils numerous ignorant church members to wrong paths. The "self-appointed Jesus" or "righteous" persons by other names also appear and lift their voices to seduce whomever they can. Now more than ever the Korean church is praying that the gift of discerning of spirits be given to all believers across the country.

Let's consider how this gift was used throughout the Old and New Testaments.

First Kings 22 relates a scene where the gift of discerning of spirits wonderfully appears. Here Ahab, the king of Israel, talked with Jehoshaphat, the king of Judah, to prepare war to take Ramoth in Gilead from Syria's hand.

At this time, Jehoshaphat and Ahab sat majestically on their thrones, having put on their robes at the entrance of the gate of Samaria. Four hundred prophets all prophesied in unison with Zedekiah the son of Chenaanah saying, "Go up to Ramoth-gilead, and prosper: for the Lord shall deliver the city into the king's hand'' (v. 12). They also made themselves horns of iron and said, ''Thus saith the Lord, With these shalt thou push the Syrians, until thou have consumed them'' (v. 11).

Jehoshaphat became a little afraid because all the prophecies were the same, so he asked Ahab whether there was any other prophet of the Lord in the land that they might inquire of him. King Ahab said that there was yet one man, Micaiah, the son of Imlay, who was a prophet, though Ahab hated him, because he always prophesied evil against him.

But King Jehoshaphat was very persistent and finally Micaiah was called in and asked about the outcome of the crusade. At first Micaiah parrotted the other prophets. But when the king, who thought that Micaiah was insincere, pressed him to speak the truth, he spoke a very negative prophecy: ''I saw all Israel scattered unto the hills, as sheep that have not a shepherd: and the Lord said, These have no master: let them return every man to his house in peace'' (v. 17). In other words, he said that Ahab would die in the battle. Then, through the wonderful gift of discerning of spirits, God showed Micaiah the hidden things that were happening in the heavens. Micaiah said:

> Hear thou therefore the word of the Lord: I saw the Lord sitting on his throne, and all the host of heaven standing by him on his right hand and on his left. And the Lord said, Who shall persuade Ahab, that he may go up and fall at Ramoth-gilead? And one said on this manner, and another said on that manner. And there came forth a spirit, and stood before the Lord, and said, I will persuade him. And the Lord said unto him, Wherewith? And he said, I will go forth, and I will be a lying spirit in the mouth of all his prophets. And he said, Thou shalt persuade him, and prevail also: go forth, and do

so. Now therefore, behold, the Lord hath put a lying spirit in the mouth of all these thy prophets, and the Lord hath spoken evil concerning thee (vv. 19-23).

By clearly revealing in a vision heavenly happenings, God enabled Micaiah, the true prophet of God, to discern the spirits.

Micaiah calmly concluded that the prophecies of the more than four hundred prophets came from the lying spirits.

God decided to allow Ahab to be killed because Ahab had persisted in rebelling and opposing Him. He allowed the evil spirits to enter the prophets of Ahab so that Ahab might be beguiled to destruction.

As we have seen from this, those who don't have the gift of discerning of spirits aren't able to distinguish which prophecy is true. Likewise, we shouldn't believe every prophecy unconditionally but discern whether a prophecy is truly spoken by the Holy Spirit or by evil spirits.

The New Testament also addresses this issue. The apostle Paul wrote of the spiritual depravity of the last times:

Even him, whose coming is after the working of Satan with all power and signs and lying wonders, and with all deceivableness of unrighteousness of them that perish; because they have received not the love of truth, that they might be saved. And for this cause God shall send them strong delusion, that they might believe a lie: That they all might be damned who believed not the truth, but had pleasure in unrighteousness (2 Thess. 2:9-12).

God allows the spirits of delusion to work among those who do not believe the Scripture—the Word of eternal truth of God—because such people insist in indulging in covetousness and delighting in unrighteousness. First Kings 22 bears clear evidence of this.

All the gifts of God should always be tested through and held up to the gift of discerning of spirits, as the more we experience the spiritual gifts, the more we should beware of lying and counterfeit spirits.

The manifestation of discerning of spirits is shown many times in the New Testament.

Since our Lord Jesus Christ is the incarnated God, the gifts of the Holy Spirit given to Him cannot be compared exactly to those given to ordinary Christians. Having said that, we can find evidence that Jesus was very interested in the discerning of spirits during His years of ministry.

In Matthew 16, when Jesus came to the coast of Caesarea Philippi, He asked His disciples, "But whom say ye that I am?" (v. 15).

When Peter quickly answered, "Thou art the Christ, the Son of the living God," Jesus answered, "Blessed art thou, Simon Bar-jona: for flesh and blood hath not revealed it unto thee, but my Father which is in heaven" (vv. 16,17).

One could think that Peter's confession of faith came from his own thoughts and belief, but Jesus made Peter discern that it was not his own thoughts; it was what God in heaven through the Holy Spirit revealed to his heart.

Later, Jesus was showing His disciples that He had to go to Jerusalem and suffer many things, even be killed and then raised again the third day. Peter's reply to this was, "Be it far from thee, Lord: this shall not be unto thee" (v. 22). This time Jesus rebuked Peter severely for what he said.

When we think of this in general terms, this "No, don't say it" of Peter's seemed to stem from his love and faithfulness to the Lord. But the Lord, through the gift of discerning of spirits, penetrated Peter's soul and said, "Get thee behind me,

Satan: thou art an offence unto me: for thou savourest not the things that be of God, but those that be of men" (v. 23).

We cannot but wonder why Peter's exhortation (which seemed to be so faithful) was in fact maneuvered behind the scene by Satan. It simply shows again how urgent the need is for the gift of discerning of spirits.

Through the experiences of Peter and Paul, the foremost servants of the Lord in the early Christian church, we can further examine the gift of discerning of spirits.

We've described Philip's crusade through Samaria (Acts 8). Many heard the gospel of Christ, received salvation and healing and were baptized. Eventually, Peter and John were asked to come and pray with these new Christians that they might receive the Holy Spirit. But a sorcerer named Simon tried to buy this gift of the Holy Spirit from Peter.

Now Simon had heard Philip's preaching and had been baptized with water. He had appeared to be a faithful believer. But when Peter saw Simon through the gift of discerning of spirits, Simon's real nature was clearly revealed. Peter said to Simon, "I perceive that thou art in the gall of bitterness, and in the bond of iniquity" (v. 23). Thus, through the gift of discerning of spirits, Simon's true colors were revealed before Peter's eyes.

A similar situation occurred in Acts 16, when Paul and Silas were in Philippi:

> And it came to pass, as we went to prayer, a certain damsel, possessed with a spirit of divination met us, which brought her masters much gain by soothsaying. The same followed Paul and us, and cried, saying, These men are the servants of the most high God, which shew unto us the way of salvation. And this did she many days. But Paul, being grieved, turned and said to the

spirit, I command thee in the name of Jesus Christ to
come out of her (vv. 16-18).

Note that when ordinary people saw the girl following Paul,
they heard her crying, "These men are the servants of the most
high God, which shew unto us the way of salvation." It was
natural that they thought that she was really helping the servants of the Lord.

But when the apostle Paul saw through this girl through the
gift of discerning of spirits, he knew that she was possessed
with a spirit of divination. Only later did Paul find out that she
made her living from divination, so it is out of the question
that he knew about her occupation through natural means. Out-
wardly she seemed to enhance the work of the gospel, but Paul
was made aware that it was actually the mischief of the devil,
so he cast out the spirit of divination. As a result Paul was beaten
and imprisoned in Philippi.

The works of the devil are continually trying to spoil the
wonderful blessings of God being poured out on today's church.
Through the manifestation of the gift of discerning of spirits
in us, we should be distinguishing the spirit of truth and the
spirit of falsehood so that we may not fall into a snare. We,
believing not every spirit, but trying the spirits whether they
are of God (see 1 John 4:1), should participate in the move-
ment of the Holy Spirit who is watchfully furthering our faith.

11

The Vocal Gifts

The gifts manifested through vocalization are the gift of tongues, the gift of interpretation of tongues and the gift of prophecy.

The Gift of Tongues

The list of gifts in 1 Corinthians 12 lists tongues: "...to another [is given] divers kinds of tongues" (v. 10).

Tongues should be placed into two categories: as a *sign* and as a *gift*.

The speaking in tongues that we previously discussed—the incidents that occurred at the time of someone's baptism with the Holy Spirit—is called the "tongue of signs," being an external proof of the inward fullness of the Holy Spirit.

THE HOLY SPIRIT, MY SENIOR PARTNER

To those who read the Bible without a preconceived theology, it is clear that all the instances of tongues recorded in Acts are this external sign of the baptism of the Holy Spirit.

The tongues listed in 1 Corinthians 12 and 14 are essentially the same as the tongues recorded in Acts, but the purpose for which they were used was different. Therefore they are called speaking in tongues "as a gift."

What is the difference? When speaking in tongues is a sign, the tongues cease after the initial baptism of the Holy Spirit. In order to continue speaking in tongues a person would subsequently receive the tongues as a gift, but in many instances people immediately possess the tongues as a gift as well as a sign.

Speaking in tongues as a gift means the tongues continue for the profit of the life of faith. Those who have received the speaking in tongues as a gift can speak in tongues anytime as they pray.

God gives the gift of tongues abundantly to accomplish several goals of faith. Let's summarize some of the reasons the gift is given:

It makes possible a deep spiritual communication with God. "For he that speaketh in an unknown tongue speaketh not unto men, but unto God: for no man understandeth him; howbeit in the spirit he speaketh mysteries" (1 Cor. 14:2). When we speak in tongues we converse directly with God, spirit to Spirit. By using this heavenly language the door is opened for us to experience the deep revelations of God.

It brings progress in one's life of faith. "He that speaketh in an unknown tongue edifieth himself" (1 Cor. 14:4). The word *edify* originally meant to lay bricks one by one in building a house. The tongue becomes the instrument by which one's own house of faith is built up.

Along with the gift of the interpretation of tongues, speaking in tongues brings forth the same effect as prophecy. "Wherefore

168

let him that speaketh in an unknown tongue pray that he may interpret'' (1 Cor. 14:13). Through the gift of interpretation, the message in tongues is understood and spoken in one's native language so that the people who hear it can be edified. Through this supernatural interpretation, they realize that the living God is with them and they gain strength in their faith.

This gift is a door to deeper prayer and praise. ''What is it then? I will pray with the spirit and I will pray with the understanding also: I will sing with the spirit, and I will sing with the understanding also'' (2 Cor. 14:15). On occasion we are moved with emotion and/or at a loss to know how to pray. At such times praying and praising the Lord in tongues can reach beyond our learned vocabulary and touch the throne of God with the most exacting description of the need or with praise that we may feel but be unable to describe.

A sign to unbelievers. ''Wherefore tongues are for a sign, not to them that believe, but to them that believe not'' (1 Cor. 14:22).

When the new wave of theology was shouting ''God is dead,'' the miracle of the vocal gifts, speaking in tongues by the Holy Spirit, came as a judgment or challenge to those heretics.

It is no wonder that the person who has received the baptism in the Holy Spirit and speaks in tongues has fervent faith and lives in victory. Summarizing those points, 1 Corinthians 14 tells us the many benefits of speaking in tongues. If we establish proper order and virtue as we use tongues in the church, the gift of tongues will become like a river of grace flowing abundantly into the hearts of believers whose experiences with the Lord have dried up.

The Gift of the Interpretation of Tongues

''...to another [is given] the interpretation of tongues'' (2 Cor. 12:10). No one can understand a message given in tongues until the meaning is revealed by God through the gift of the interpretation of tongues.

The Bible reads, "For he that speaketh in an unknown tongue speaketh not unto men, but unto God: for no man understandeth him; howbeit in the spirit he speaketh mysteries" (1 Cor. 14:2). Later Paul says, "Wherefore let him that speaketh in an unknown tongue pray that he may interpret" (1 Cor. 14:13).

Interpretation of tongues is different from an ordinary translation. Translation generally gives the word-for-word meaning of a foreign language, while interpretation makes clear the overall meaning of a foreign language. For instance, a message in tongues may be short, while the interpretation of it is long. At other times the message in tongues is long but the interpretation is short.

Since the interpretation of tongues is a gift of God manifested through man, we should not regard it as being equal with the Bible.

Much caution is needed and the interpretation of tongues should be discerned. The interpretation of tongues largely depends upon the interpreter's condition of faith, prayer life and depth of spiritual communication with God. There can also be times when the personal thoughts of an interpreter or the interference of the devil influences the interpretation.

Like any other gift, the gift of the interpretation of tongues is manifested through the miracle of the inspiration of the Holy Spirit. No one can interpret messages in tongues continually as he could if he were translating a foreign language.

Interpretation of tongues is possible only when God allows the inspiration of the interpretation. Occasionally, I have seen tongues-speaking people lined up to interpret a series of messages, boasting that they can interpret every message given. This is false and very dangerous.

I can best discuss the process of the interpretation of tongues by writing of my own experiences.

After I received the gift of speaking in tongues, in accordance with the teaching of the Scriptures, I kept praying earnestly that I might receive the gift of interpretation.

One day in my room in the dormitory, after having attended an early-morning prayer meeting, I began to pray privately in tongues. Suddenly the whole room seemed brighter. When I opened my eyes the room was still dark, but when I closed them again it seemed as if the sun were shining. Then the interpretation of tongues began to pour out from my lips.

Out of tremendous joy, I abused the gift of the interpretation of tongues in the days ahead and committed many errors. But after graduation from Bible college until now, the interpretation of tongues has become an incomparable treasure in my Christian experience. Like everything else, this gift has improved and settled more and more through the accumulated experiences of time, so that now I possess considerable discernment, for which I thank God.

From my personal experiences as well as those of well-known Spirit-filled leaders, the gift of the interpretation of tongues can be manifested in several ways:

First, a person interpreting a message given in tongues sometimes interprets only by faith through the commandment of the Holy Spirit in his heart, which is like a sudden urging in his spirit. At such a time, the powerful commandment of God fills the heart together with the abundant grace of the Holy Spirit. Then, as Abraham, who in accordance with the calling of God went out of Ur of the Chaldees not knowing where he was to go, the person begins to speak by faith and mysteriously God provides the ability to interpret the message.

Second, when someone gives a message in tongues there will

be times when only the general meaning of it is revealed to a heart. In this case every word of the message is not known. At such a time the person who received the interpretation by the Holy Spirit explains it with his own knowledge and words.

Third, when someone speaks in tongues, sometimes only a part of the message in tongues is revealed. If that part is verbalized, the remaining part is then revealed, like an unwinding spool of thread. As we continue on, the interpretation unfolds.

Fourth, right after a message in tongues is given, the interpretation of it may follow immediately through the same person, flowing as freely as did the message in tongues. In this case, the interpretation is given only to the mouth (the person doesn't mentally form the words) with the interpretation flowing out as long as the inspiration of the Holy Spirit continues.

Finally, there is a case in which a message spoken in a foreign tongue is heard in the vernacular language which everyone can understand. This rarely happens but I have heard several testimonies of the experience.

The Gift of Prophecy

"...to another [is given] prophecy" (1 Cor. 12:10). When we say the word *prophecy*, we understand it literally as the revealed word of God about the future.

Through the Old and New Testaments God prophesied of the end of history, of the new heaven and the new earth centering around the people of Israel.

All these prophecies written in the Bible are the Word of God handed down to us through the accurate record of the prophets who wrote by the inspiration of the Holy Spirit.

Note what the apostle Peter wrote, "For the prophecy came not in old time by the will of man: but holy men of God spake as they were moved by the Holy Ghost" (2 Pet. 1:21).

By His special providence, God overshadowed the scriptural prophecies and writings so that they were recorded without flaw until the canon (the books of the Bible officially accepted as genuine) was established.

Because the Bible has already been completed, the prophecy given as a gift of the Holy Spirit is different from the scriptural prophecies. The main purpose for the prophecy given under the anointing of the Holy Spirit today is not to foretell future events, but to edify, exhort and comfort believers. The Bible clearly teaches: "But he that prophesieth speaketh unto men to edification, and exhortation, and comfort" (1 Cor. 14:3).

Concerning this gift of prophecy, I do not mean to say that this gift does not relate to future events. Rather, I mean that the word of prophecy resulting from a manifestation of this gift can never be considered equal to or take the place of the written Word of God. Also, even though a prophecy may be spoken by a person who has received this gift, the truthfulness or falsehood of the prophecy should be discerned and judged by other believers.

Paul confirmed this in his epistle to the Corinthians, "Let the prophets speak two or three, and let the other judge" (1 Cor. 14:29). Again, the prophecy manifested today as the gift of the Holy Spirit should not be accepted blindly but received with discernment.

This is also clear from Isaiah 8:20: "To the law and to the testimony: if they speak not according to this word, it is because there is no light in them."

Today's prophecy is to confirm that believers can accept the lessons and word of biblical prophecy and receive salvation in accordance with the teachings of the Bible, going into deeper faith.

The apostle Paul wrote concerning prophecy being used in

the church: "But if all prophesy, and there come in one that believeth not, or one unlearned, he is convinced of all, he is judged of all: And thus are the secrets of his heart made manifest; and so falling down on his face, he will worship God, and report that God is in you of a truth" (1 Cor. 14:24,25).

Here again the gift of prophecy is described in terms of ministry—convincing of sin, judging a mischievous life or manifesting the secrets of the heart. As a result, a person's faith will be edified and the church, the body of Jesus Christ, will grow.

Because of such characteristics of prophecy, Paul, of all the gifts, especially emphasized prophecy and said, "Desire spiritual gifts, but rather that ye may prophesy" (1 Cor. 14:1), and "Wherefore, brethren, covet to prophesy, and forbid not to speak with tongues" (1 Cor. 14:39).

Prophecy is the gift that today's ministers and preachers of the gospel of Jesus Christ should especially desire. When the Word is preached through such a gift to a congregation, the invigorating power appears and the fruit of the gospel can be harvested.

Many people today misuse or abuse this gift. Having departed from the teachings of the gospel, they habitually foretell other people's fortunes like a fortune-teller.

Such people have not received the true gift of the Holy Spirit but are possessed by lying spirits and have become prophets of evil spirits of divination. As with all other gifts, the gift of prophecy is given only to preach the gospel of Christ and to edify the church; by no means is it given to fulfill a personal desire or as an instrument of distinction. Those who have received the gift of prophecy, by the inspiration of the Holy Spirit, should use this gift only for the preaching of the gospel and for the saving of lost souls.

12

The Gifts of Power

So far we have studied the gifts of revelation (the word of wisdom, the word of knowledge and discerning of spirits) and the gifts of vocalization (tongues, the interpretation of tongues and prophecy). Now let us look into the gifts of power.

The Gift of Faith

"To another [is given] faith by the same Spirit" (1 Cor. 12:9).

Faith is the treasure without which man cannot live. Suppose you lost your faith even for a moment. You would doubt the faithfulness of your family members. You would not be able to drive your automobile or ride other means of transportation, for you would doubt them. By mistrusting the facilities that are essential to our civilized life—such as banks or post offices—your whole life would be completely paralyzed.

As a person is born with eyes, ears, nose and mouth, so he or she is born with faith. Some people develop this faith more rapidly than others. With great conviction in life they ceaselessly keep it growing, while others become more shriveled and negative.

But let's think about Christian faith and belief. Nowadays, such expressions as "I don't have any faith" and "I have little faith" often leave the mouths of Christians.

Is there really one who doesn't have any faith? Romans 12:3 says that we are "to think soberly, according as God hath dealt to every man the measure of faith." This verse reveals clearly that God has imparted to every man a measure of faith. If this is true, then why don't people admit that they have received it? God never lies. Therefore, though there may be a difference of degree in faith, no one among those who have accepted Jesus Christ as Savior is totally faithless. So in obedience to the Word of God, we should say, "I have faith as written in the Scripture. I have enough faith to be saved, to receive healing and to get answers from God."

Moreover, the faith we received from God in the Lord grows when we hear the Word of God. In Romans 10:17 we read, "So then faith cometh by hearing, and hearing by the word of God." When we hear the Word of God, meditate on it and digest it, we receive faith. And that faith grows.

Some believers might say, "My faith seems to be so weak." Though God did not praise anyone's weak faith, He never said that weak faith is good for nothing. Jesus said in Matthew 17:20, "For verily I say unto you, If ye have faith as a grain of mustard seed, ye shall say unto this mountain, Remove hence to yonder place; and it shall remove; and nothing shall be impossible unto you."

This word teaches that it is not important whether your faith is strong or weak, great or small, but whether you have a living or a dead faith. Faith as small as a mustard seed—living, working and believing in the miracles of God—will produce great power beyond human imagination.

So far in this discussion, we have considered general faith and the faith God deals to us according to our measure and the faith produced by the Word. But how is the *gift* of faith manifested by the Holy Spirit?

The gift of faith given by the Holy Spirit has characteristics very different from the other types of faith mentioned above. Faith given as a gift is itself the direct and immediate work of the Holy Spirit, and it means that divine faith is deposited in the heart of the believer. This strong and keen faith, beyond human imagining, is produced so that great miracles may be performed by God.

This faith is not possessed by a believer permanently, but is manifested through the believer when a need arises in accordance with the Holy Spirit's time and place.

I have experienced this particular faith many times. At a time of need the Holy Spirit sheds in my heart the gift of faith to accomplish God's glorious work. Whenever I experience this imparted gift of faith, with supernatural passion and mental concentration I come to believe that God is in control and as a result the answer to my need follows.

The Gift of Healing

"...to another [is given] the gifts of healing by the same Spirit" (1 Cor. 12:9). Christian faith and healing are inseparable. Actually, healing is a central part of the gospel of the redeeming grace of the Lord Jesus Christ.

In the Old Testament, God is revealed as the healing God.

Exodus records God's making a covenant with the children of Israel:

> If thou wilt diligently hearken to the voice of the Lord thy God, and wilt do that which is right in his sight, and wilt give ear to his commandments, and keep all his statutes, I will put none of these diseases upon thee, which I have brought upon the Egyptians: for I am the Lord that healeth thee (Ex. 15:26).

David, the king chosen by God to lead His people, praised God and said, "Who forgiveth all thine iniquities; who healeth all thy diseases" (Ps. 103:3).

Malachi, the writer of the last book of the Old Testament, prophesied saying, "But unto you that fear my name shall the Sun of righteousness arise with healing in his wings" (4:2). This showed that the work of evangelism of Jesus Christ would be the work of healing both the spirit and the flesh.

The public ministry of Jesus was truly the life of healing. Nearly two-thirds of Jesus' ministry was filled with the works of healing.

Isaiah, who prophesied about 700 B.C., described the redemption of Jesus. In Isaiah 53, he detailed the redeeming work of Jesus Christ and stressed that sickness and disease were included in the sufferings of the redemptive work: "Surely he hath borne our griefs, and carried our sorrows" (v. 4); "And with his stripes we are healed" (v. 5); "Yet it pleased the Lord to bruise him; he hath put him to grief" (v. 10).

The truths of these prophecies were all verified by the testimonies of Jesus' disciples. Matthew, after recording the wonderful works of healing by Jesus, acknowledged that this was in fact the accomplishment of Isaiah 53:4: "[He] healed all that were sick: That it might be fulfilled which was spoken by Esaias the prophet, saying, Himself took our infirmities, and bare our sicknesses'' (Matt. 8:16,17).

Peter, recording the redemption of Jesus, did not fail to include that the healing we receive from Jesus was a part of Jesus' suffering for the redemption of mankind: ''By whose stripes ye were healed'' (1 Pet. 2:24).

Then the last and greatest commandment of Jesus, given just before ascending into heaven, concerned the casting out of devils and healing (see Mark 16:15-18). Here He clearly said that healing was inseparable from the preaching of the gospel.

The Gift of the Working of Miracles

''To another [is given] the working of miracles'' (1 Cor. 12:10). The word *miracle* refers to a remarkable or surprising event that happens by the direct intervention of God, not following the generally known laws of nature. A miracle is the temporary suspension of the usual laws of nature and the intervention of supernatural and divine power. The Bible contains an extensive record of such miracles.

The Old Testament includes miracles in almost every book. Let us examine some of these recordings.

The most famous example is the miracle God performed in the lives of Abraham and Sarah. When Abraham was about a hundred years old and Sarah was well past the age when she could conceive, God miraculously gave them a son, Isaac, who became the forefather of the Jewish nation.

This miracle was so wonderful that the New Testament describes it thus:

Who [Abraham] against hope believed in hope....And being not weak in faith, he considered not his own body now dead, when he was about an hundred years old,

179

neither yet the deadness of Sarah's womb: he staggered not at the promise of God through unbelief; but was strong in faith, giving glory to God; and being fully persuaded that, what he had promised, he was able to perform (Rom. 4:18-22).

This faith for the working of miracles was given not only to Abraham but also to Sarah:

Through faith also Sarah herself received strength to conceive seed, and was delivered of a child when she was past age, because she judged him faithful who had promised. Therefore sprang there even of one, and him as good as dead, so many as the stars of the sky in multitude, and as the sand which is by the sea shore innumerable (Heb. 11:11,12).

Such an occurrence is not common. It is the miracle that, through the special intervention of God, brought about a conception that was totally impossible by natural laws.

Another miracle occurred when Moses and the children of Israel came to the shores of the Red Sea. They were blocked by the sea to the front and a great army of Egyptian soldiers to the rear. When Moses prayed to God, the answer was given to him. With a rod in his right hand Moses commanded the water of the Red Sea to part and the children of Israel proceeded to walk through the sea as if it were dry ground.

Some opponents insist that this was not a miracle at all. They claim that when Moses came to the Red Sea, the tide subsided so he "luckily" could go into the midst of it.

These people, however, disregard the fact that the Egyptians who pursued Israel all drowned in the water. If the water had been shallow enough for the children of Israel to enter and cross, why were the whole Egyptian army and its horses killed?

By the law of nature the sea could not be divided so the people could cross over on dry ground. Such a phenomenon can happen only by the power of God manifesting itself over the law of nature: a miracle.

Other wonderful manifestations of the gift of the working of miracles took place in the life of Joshua. Joshua was leading the children of Israel in a fierce battle against the Amorites. To win, the Israelites needed time, but the sun began to set. Suddenly Joshua lifted up his voice, looked at the sun and cried: "Sun, stand thou still upon Gibeon; and thou Moon, in the valley of Analon" (Josh. 10:12). The gift of the working of miracles operated through Joshua right there.

From the human viewpoint, what a foolish cry! Yet the Bible records the results: "And the sun stood still, and the moon stayed, until the people had avenged themselves upon their enemies. Is not this written in the book of Jasher? So the sun stood still in the midst of heaven, and hasted not to go down about a whole day" (Josh. 10:13).

Again, God suspended temporarily the operation of natural law to manifest His divine providence.

The New Testament also records numerous cases of the manifestation of the gift of the working of miracles.

The healing that we receive when we come to the Lord falls into two categories: Some comes by the gift of healing and some by the gift of the working of miracles.

When the gift of the working of miracles works, the disease departs in a moment and the person immediately begins to recover health. When the gift of healing works, the cause of the disease is removed slowly and the effect of treatment starts to work, leading to recovery.

Conclusion

When the great work of the Holy Spirit begins to take over, established churches often persecute the work of the Holy Spirit. But Christians must stand firm against wrong doctrines or heresies that arise against or imitate the work of the Holy Spirit. For the Holy Spirit to be free to be manifested more, we must maintain a healthy, strong faith based on the Word of God. And for this a basic understanding of the doctrine of the Holy Spirit is indispensable.

For this purpose, this book was written to enlighten, teach and encourage believers as they prepare their hearts in prayer for the greatest move of the Holy Spirit—yet to come!